REFLECTIONS ON RISK

ASA INSTITUTE FOR RESEARCH AND INNOVATION

ANNIE SEARLE & ASSOCIATES LLC

TAUTEGORY PRESS
SEATTLE, WASHINGTON

Printed in the United States of America

First edition: February 2012

Tautegory Press, Seattle, Washington USA

Printing History
All research notes here were previously published as "ASA Research Notes" in ASA Newsletters ©Annie Searle & Associates LLC and at its website *http://www.anniesearle.com* [November 2009 – January 2012]

USA Library of Congress Control Number: 2012931422
ISBN # 978-0-9839347-2-1

Cover design by Jesse Brown
Typography by Stephanie Martindale

Contents

Acknowledgements

I am extremely proud of the work that all four of these research associates have done, and for the time they took to review their original research notes for this volume. I'd like to thank our current research associate, Andrew Hansen, for his compilation and review of the 22 research notes to bring them to this point. Jesse Brown designed the cover, the second that he has collaborated with me on; and Stephanie Martindale handled the interior typography.

The direction of our research has been informed by my affiliation with New York University's Global Risk Forum since 2007; and by ASA's Institute for Risk and Innovation's participation since 2009. The forum has provided a rich mix of public and private sector perspectives on operational risk priorities.

Finally, I'd like to thank Mike Crandall from the University of Washington's Information School for a strong internship partnership that benefits both the university and this firm.

Introduction

When I founded Annie Searle & Associates LLC in the spring of 2009, I was determined to provide world class operational risk consulting services to businesses of all sizes, but in particular to critical infrastructure sectors like banking and finance, energy, telecommunications, information technology, public health, and emergency services. Those are areas upon which the resilience of our country depends.

In my previous position at Washington Mutual, I had worked on national task forces with representatives of most of these sectors, examining operational challenges that we all faced: the security of corporate data and personal information; the challenges to privacy with new legislation designed to counter terrorism; the gaps in a coordinated response to natural disasters like Hurricane Katrina that caused billions of dollars of loss; the advent of social media tools that can burnish or destroy corporate reputations; the rise of a cyber-terrorism; and the increasingly precarious state of our global supply chain.

Annie Searle & Associates LLC – also known as ASA – is organized into six practice areas that build upon my own experience on national projects: global response, business practices, information technology, business continuity, corporate security, and information security. All six areas roll up to the larger category of "operational risk."

Operational risk differs from credit or market risk. It is present in every organization, and exists because of the intersection of people, systems, business processes, and external events. Information analysis – or the lack of it – is a critical element in operational risk management, to ensure that important business processes and behaviors stay within the tolerances that have been established in an organization. Operational risk management involves monitoring internal controls to minimize the possibility of loss from internal or external fraud; legal and liability loss; noncompliance with regulations; processing errors; physical security breaches; information security breaches, technology failures, disaster recovery and continuity of operations events. In another article, I argued that

> "Relying simply upon color coded executive reports has not solved certain types of problems that have plagued us for the past several years, particularly in the financial marketplace—but also in other critical infrastructure sectors that also rely upon disciplines such as information and physical security, audit and compliance, internal and external fraud, and business continuity/ disaster recovery.
>
> All critical infrastructure sectors need to be looking past obvious risks to those which are unknown or hidden, or where complacency has set in."[1]

I argued in that same paper that "operational risk deserves a place at the table whenever corporate strategic planning and risk identification is taking place, not just in the midst of a "real disaster."[2] Knowing the importance of research in improving operational risk practices, I designed the firm, also known as ASA, to have two divisions. The first is an exceptional risk consulting practice; and the other an Institute for Risk and Innovation, which publishes risk-related research through a variety of channels and which informs our consulting practice. We created the monthly ASA newsletter in November of 2009. I laid out the publication's charter in that first issue. I welcomed readers to

> "ASA's Institute for Risk and Innovation, where we are analyzing these issues, working to impact regulatory reform and public policy, knowing there must be a better way to think about and manage risk at the operational level in companies of all sizes.
>
> We'll try to summarize some of the Institute's work here each month. You'll find links to media stories, upcoming conferences, calls for papers, and to ASA Research Notes which often include best practices around risk."[3]

I should explain at the outset that ASA Research Notes are not full research papers: they are examinations of a single topic with commentary in a short, digestible format, designed to be readable by executives or experts.

ASA could not have published such a content-rich newsletter with new research topics each month were it not for a unique relationship set up with the University of Washington's Information School. From a number of qualified applicants each year, I select an academic year intern, and a summer program intern, who compile and edit the newsletter, and contribute a research note to each issue in addition to their other responsibilities.

All four of the research associates, described on the contributors' page, were second year students in the Master of Science in Information Management (MSIM) program in the University of Washington's Information School when they performed their ASA internships. The consistently high quality of the research notes is due to an open approach to the topics being examined. The associates perform extensive research, and then form well-grounded conclusions and recommendations for a reading audience that includes risk professionals as well as academics and executives.

Each research note is published first in the newsletter, and then to the "Research" section of the ASA website. This volume makes all of the work to date available to a broader audience.

References

1. Searle, Annie. "A Seat at the Table for Operational Risk," *Proceedings of the 7th International ISCRAM Conference*, Seattle, USA, May 2010, p. 1. *<http://www.scribd.com/doc/35645370/ISCRAM2010Proceedings-with AbstractsandLinkstoFullPapers>*

2. Searle, p. 2.

3. Searle, Annie. "Why an Institute of Risk and Innovation." *Annie Searle & Associates, LLC.* 10 Nov. 2009. Newsletter. *<http://anniesearle. createsend.com/t/ViewEmailArchive/r/C8BF11470718B603/ C67FD2F38AC4859C/>*

The Contributors

Akshay Bhagwatwar joined ASA in the fall of 2009. As the first Research Associate to join the ASA Institute for Risk and Innovation, Akshay published four research notes, and designed and launched the ASA newsletter in December of 2009. Akshay received his Bachelor of Engineering from the University of Mumbai, majoring in Information Technology. He received his Master of Science in Information Management (MSIM) degree from the UW Information School in June of 2010, and is now a PhD candidate at Indiana University's highly esteemed business school. You can read more about his research interests and studies at *www.akshayb.com*.

Shirish K. Munshi joined ASA for a summer internship in June of 2010, and is the author of three research notes. He produced three issues of the ASA newsletter and completed focused research for ASA clients. He is a graduate of the University of Mumbai, with a degree in engineering and IT. He received his Master of Science in Information Management (MSIM) in the spring of 2011 from the UW Information School, and is now part of the information security practice of a national consulting firm.

Emily J. Oxenford joined ASA for the academic year 2010-2011 and is the author of nine research notes. Emily received her B.A. in International Studies from American University, graduating cum laude with a concentration in

Peace & Conflict Resolution. She received her Master of Science in Information Management (MSIM) in the spring of 2011 from the University of Washington, and then accepted a research analyst position with a Seattle-based public accounting and consulting firm. She now conducts research and analysis projects across firm service groups including assurance, tax, consulting, risk management, transaction, and wealth services.

Andrew H. R. Hansen joined ASA for the 2011-2012 academic year and is the author of four research notes. He holds a Bachelor of Science degree in Information Systems from the University of Utah, and is a second year student in the University of Washington's Master of Science in Information Management (MSIM) program. He completed a summer internship at The Boeing Company in 2011, and is a skilled researcher with prior experience at H-11 Digital Forensics and the State of Utah.

Annie Searle is the founder and principal of Annie Searle & Associates LLC. She has two degrees in literature from the University of Iowa. She is an affiliate faculty member at the University of Washington in the School of Information, the author of one book and a number of articles concerned with elements of operational risk.

Chapter I

Business Practices

In this research note, I address the streamlining of corporate controls as organizations evolve, particularly in the area of technology platform or application controls. Often we find a mix of applications, some of which may be operated by the business and only secondarily supported by the technology group, with a mix of manual and automated processes that make them difficult to streamline, much less to measure. The result is that, even though controls are in place and reports are being generated, the operational risk around technology controls is still high.

Simpler Internal Controls

Annie Searle
November 2009

Well-known management expert Rosabeth Moss Kanter has a new publication called "Simplicity: The Next Big Thing," in which she weighs in on streamlined design, fewer products and less-complex processes for one's customers.[1] Some companies have already adapted a Six Sigma disciplined approach, originally derived from cleaning up and "leaning out" manufacturing processes. Here, we'll take a quick look at how operational risk controls can be strengthened by working across operations or platforms that are silos, to effectively streamline and simplify the environment.

A hard look at IT platforms, policies or procedures usually finds a significant amount of layering over time. Rather than tweak the technology platform architecture when an application is added to the environment, the new application often sits inconsistently in the production environment. In the IT world in particular, this can create a nearly unmanageable environment when the applications do not play well with one another, or use "customized" controls to allow for idiosyncrasies in the environment.

If we look more broadly to the advent of Enterprise Risk Management (ERM) tools, we see another variant of customized controls: in order to deal with various technology applications and platforms in the environment, the tool itself becomes so customized as to be unable to measure anything in a meaningful way. Instead it simply reports the pre-established controls around the application. An intention to measure across the enterprise is therefore thwarted.

A good example of an un-streamlined environment can be seen in the disparity between the uniformity and tightness of mainframe controls and the level of controls variation on distributed systems platforms. To adequately protect consumers and customers who shop or bank on the Internet is a true controls challenge because data passes through both the mainframe and the distributed systems platform, where design must be well engineered to both protect against and anticipate threats from Internet fraudsters that have not yet materialized.

Often an audit or regulatory "finding" is a result of a disconnect. It may be related to a company's formal governance process (including policies and standards and reporting around internal controls) or it may be in how certain types of work are performed (operational processes and procedures and reporting). Sometimes the disconnect is unintentional, perhaps the result of a lack of staff training. And sometimes the control itself is so manual that it is easy to deliberately ignore it, especially if employees are impatient or annoyed with the right way to do things.

In the operational risk arena, key internal controls as identified by the Federal Financial Institutions Examination Council (FFIEC) include:

- Creation and safe storage of records
- Adequate segregation of duties among those responsible for the control
- Reliable MIS data with complete auditable cycles
- Efficient and effective operating procedures
- Procedures for business continuity
- Identification and monitoring of high risks with reports to executives
- Adherence to management standards and policies, applicable laws and regulations, regulatory policies and guidelines[2]

Though the FFIEC guidance is written specifically for the banking and finance sector, these areas of control are applicable to most other regulated sectors as well, such as IT, communications, and energy. As seen from the recent financial crisis, to manage risk effectively means looking at the big picture, not just narrowly at individual controls. Though he was writing specifically about market and credit risk, the six errors identified by Rene M. Stultz in a March 2009 Harvard Business Review article are applicable to operational risk as well. All of these errors are a result of looking too narrowly at operational risk, especially if there is not a coherent and streamlined controls design at the enterprise level that looks across all of the silos to aggregate the risk(s).

Here are the six errors that Stultz identifies:

- Relying upon historical data

- Focusing on narrow measures

- Overlooking knowable risks

- Overlooking concealed risks

- Failing to communicate

- Not managing in real time.[3]

A first step that every institution can take is to examine the incongruities and unnecessary complexities in its existing control structure; and to ensure that there is a specific senior group assigned to handle enterprise risk management inside the company.

References

1. Kanter, Rosabeth Moss. "Cut Your Company's Complexity," *Harvard Business Management* Tip Of the Day, July 7, 2009

2. FFIEC Examination Handbook Infobase, *http://ithandbook.ffiec.gov/it-booklets/audit/it-audit-roles-and-responsibilities/board-of-directors-and-senior-management.aspx*

3. Stultz, Rene M. "Six Ways Companies Mismanage Risk," *Harvard Business Review* 87.3 (2009): Web. Mar. 2009. *<http://hbr.org/2009/03/six-ways-companies-mismanage-risk/ar/1>*

This note was written late in 2010 after WikiLeaks had released over a quarter of a million State Department cables that contained privileged information, much of it written in language that was often unflattering and which, in some cases, compromised the identities of diplomatic partners being described. In this research note, I argue that our national data classification system needs to be brought into the 21st century with a review of what is genuinely sensitive data.

Diplomacy and the Law

Annie Searle
December 2010

We are in the midst of an information war of sorts, fueled by the close relationship between WikiLeaks and the media, at a time in our history where there has been no real adjustment of law or policy to deal with the digital world we live in except for controls now in place around nonpublic personal information via the Gramm-Leach-Bliley Act (GLBA); or the Health Insurance Portability and Accountability Act (HIPAA) controls that are designed to protect patients' personal information.

Against the First Amendment right to free speech, which since the Federalist papers includes the right to publish anonymously, we are looking at a system of data classification that may need to be updated, when sensitive information of various types is restricted by law or regulation.

Most every government, including our own, uses a system involving secrecy that requires different levels of clearance for access. Information security policies in many private corporations and organizations also provide a scheme by which sensitive information is classified, often for purposes having to do with intellectual property, mergers, acquisitions, trade secrets, legal issues and/or quarterly financial disclosures. Like the government, the private sector prosecutes those against which a case can be made for what here is generally considered a form of internal fraud.

In this country, national security classifications range from the highest level ("Top Secret") down four more levels to the lowest ("Unclassified"). An organization like WikiLeaks is a metaphorical "drop box" for those who have security clearances sufficient to have access to sensitive data, and who feel that there is a reason to make the information public. It is very clear that law and regulation is designed to protect sensitive documents, but it is not so clear – especially in the escalated rhetoric of the present "Cablegate" situation – who is at fault, and who should be prosecuted.

As Evgeny Morozov points out in his New York Times article titled "Why it's Hard to Duplicate," Cablegate is a watershed event.[1] Diplomatic cables, like explosive videos or photographs, do not appear to need much explanation – even as to why they were highly classified. Yet without investigative reporting and some context in which to better understand the meaning and impact, the only thing that changes is the advice that authors of diplomatic cables will receive on how to write their reports.

If the National Security Administration has its way, there will be an attempt to revert to stove-piped information that is highly controlled and thought to be secure.

Perhaps Cablegate will be the tipping point for a review of our current data classification scheme as well as the laws and regulations that surround sensitive documents. At the same time, greater care must be taken by organizations like WikiLeaks to ensure that the information they release does not inadvertently end up compromising the identities of actual people, such as Saudi princes or even dissidents who shared their views with the State Department.

In the meantime, in a twist upon the old saying, it's best to remember never to say (or write) something you wouldn't be embarrassed to read in tomorrow's newspaper.

References

1.   Morozov, Evgeny. "Why It's Hard to Duplicate," part of "What Has WikiLeaks Started," *New York Times* editorial, December 10, 2010. Print.

Oxenford argues that small businesses can benefit from information audits, especially as they start to grow. This is not just an academic research note. In completion of requirements for the MSIM degree, Oxenford put the recommendations in this note into practice by performing an information and risk assessment of Annie Searle & Associates LLC. As a result, ASA's own information handling practices have been improved.

Information Needs and Using Information Audits

Emily Oxenford
February 2011

Introduction

Starting and running a small business is no easy task. There are almost countless challenges, decisions, and considerations on a daily basis that must be handled adroitly by small-business owners and employees. But one thing that most businesses share is the goal to expand and grow into a stronger, better organization. A key way to move a business forward towards reaching that goal is to identify the organizational information needs, and how those can be met. One approach is to perform an information audit on your organization.

Information Audit as Assessment

So what does that mean? There are a wide variety of meanings that can be associated with "information audit," such as "information needs," "information assessment" and "information workflow." It is important to understand that there are some discrepancies between understandings of what these terms mean, and different applications depending on the approach taken. There is a definite lack of industry definitions as well – an "information audit" might mean something completely different to a financial institution compared to a public hospital or small IT business. There is generally a more technical connotation associated with the term information audit – an examination of information systems versus the holistic flow of information throughout an organization. A useful definition for an information audit is that crafted by Botha & Boon:

> "An information audit entails the systematic examination of the information resources, information use, information flows and the management of these in an organization. It involves the identification of users' information needs and how effectively (or not) these are being met. In addition to this, the (monetary) cost and the value of the information resources to the organization are calculated and determined. All this is done with a view to determining whether the organizational information environment contributes to the attainment of the organizational objectives and furthermore, to the establishment and implementation of effective information management principles and procedures. This is done so that information can be used to help the organization maintain its competitive edge."[1]

This definition is useful for different organizations because it is holistic enough to include the non-system sources of information within the firm. The purpose aligns as well with business goals, since the audit, as stated by Botha and Boon, is meant to allow for increasing a competitive edge and further organizational initiatives.

Identifying Information Resources

An information audit can cover a variety of information resources and information sources at a business. Firstly, there is the internal information within the organization itself. This can include everything from the operational and strategic information – from website content to style documentation, financial data and future planning. There is also tacit information made up of an employee's professional network, and the explicit content produced for clients and the press.[2]

Other types of information that might be important include relevant industry information, competitive information, and government information. Industry information can be knowledge about business best practices, trends, and other resources within the industry and organization associates. A business also wants to know what competitive information it possesses, keeping up with what competitors are doing and producing. Finally, it is important for some businesses to know about government requirements and standards, but in general there are simply just many resources for small businesses available from the federal government.[3]

Why an Information Audit

According to Botha and Boon, "the main aim of an information audit is specific to the environment in which it is performed. If one were to attempt to generalise the aim of an information audit, it could be said that an information audit would be performed with the purpose of collecting the information that is needed to manage organisational information resources effectively, so that organisational objectives are met."[4]

How to Do an Information Audit

There are a number of aspects that must be considered when undertaking an information needs assessment through an audit. Unfortunately, there are no universal rules or guidelines for performing audits that can be applied across organizations. The organizational environment and context will determine what kind of approach can be taken for an audit, what direction it takes, and what the final product looks like. Ultimately, an information audit needs to be defined by the mission, goals and functions of an organization. A critical prerequisite developing the direction and methodology for an information audit is "a clearly defined scope and purpose."[5]

While there is no standard set of activities or approaches for an information assessment, there are a few generalizations that can be made. The following recommendations are adapted from Botha and Boon.[6]

Prerequisites

There are a few elements that should be present before a business implements an information audit. There should be:

- Support from top management

- Skilled staff to conduct the assessment and the audit, or resources to hire consultants to conduct the audit
- Sufficient time to complete the research, and time to follow-up on recommendations
- Free access to relevant information and the right people
- A culture of acceptance of the audit by employees.

Stages

Many information audits go through the following stages.

- Planning of the audit itself
- Performing an information needs assessment
- Conducting an information inventory
- Costing and valuing information resources
- Analysis of findings
- Producing final report (with recommendations).

Activities

There are a few general activities that are often used during an information audit.

- Defining the organizational environment
- Data collection (by conducting a physical tour and/or obtaining relevant documentation and/or interviews and analysis of the collected information)
- The identification of strong and weak points

- The compilation of the final report and the presentation of the findings to management.

Conclusion

The value of doing an information needs assessment can come from a variety of results. Closing information gaps within a business can make processes more efficient, create clearer lines of communication, and strengthen the information foundation. It is important to tailor the approach to the needs of an organization, so that the audit process is informed by the identified business needs of the firm.

References

1. Botha, Hanneri, and J.A. Boon. "The Information Audit: Principles and Guidelines." *Libri* 53 (2002): p. 23-38. Web 19 Dec. 2011. p. 24. *<http://www.librijournal.org/pdf/2003-1pp23-38.pdf>*

2. Richards, Leigh. "What Types of Information Resources Does a Business Usually Need? "n.d. n. pag. Web. Feb 2011. *<http://smallbusiness.chron.com/types-information-resources-business-usually-need-4753.html>*

3. Richards, n. pag.

4. Botha & Boon, p. 24.

5. Buchanan, S. and Gibb, F. "The Information Audit: an Integrated Strategic Approach." *International Journal of Information Management* 18.1 (1998):29–47.

6. The following have been adapted from Botha & Boon.

From my June 2011 column, in support of Oxenford's research note: "Brand and reputational risk management depend upon the external perceptions of employees, customers, consumers, constituents, and/or shareholders. Whether personal or corporate, reputational risk management seeks to increase softer perceptions based on attributes like trust and authenticity... describe your products and services as accurately as possible. Don't overpromise and under-deliver or you will find your reputational risk exposure to be off the charts. Companies (and politicians) have gone out of business on this one type of risk."

Branding and Managing Reputational Risk

Emily Oxenford
June 2011

Introduction

Billionaire businessman Warren Buffett once said, "It takes 20 years to build a reputation and five minutes to ruin it."[1] And we have seen the truth of that in recent years. There have been many well-established organizations and individuals that have faced defining moments that, depending on the choices made, determined survival beyond that key turning point. It is how organizations prepare for and handle these moments that define their future reputations.

While everyone knows that there are many dangers and risks that exist in the world, the risks associated with reputation and brand can be particularly tricky. This stems from the fact that while there are actions for strengthening and protecting a reputation, ultimately the power to control reputation rests in the hands of others. Organizations and individuals are increasingly recognizing the critical importance of preparing for and facing these risks, particularly in the age of instant and easily replicable communication.

Brand and Reputation

The ideas of brand and reputation are certainly related to each other, though there are a few distinctions that can be made between the two. While there is not universal agreement about what these differences necessarily are, it is important for an organization to think the two parts through.

Reputation can be summed up as the ideas, beliefs, expectations, and opinions that are held (in general) about something or someone. The perception of an organization does not necessarily have to be based on truth or reality, but is simply the way that someone or something is thought about by others. And reputation has been shown to be an escalating factor in both business value and customer behavior. One report found that the intangibles like reputation actually account for a majority of organizational assets, particularly in service-oriented firms.[2]

Brand, on the other hand, is not as neatly summed up. Maria Ross writes that brand can be thought of as "the personality and soul of an organization communicated in various ways."[3] Bill Taylor talks about for an organization "your brand is your culture, your culture is your brand,"[4] in the sense that internal factors can play just as an important part of building external brand as the other brand initiatives. An organization does in general have more control over building and shaping brand. But brand is not simply good public relations or a strong marketing campaign, but rather all the interactions and actions of an organization both internally and externally. Brand is part of reputation, and a well-developed brand can help protect reputation in times of crisis and business interruptions. Building a clear and consistent brand is critical especially for businesses, Ross stresses. "Brand clarity attracts customers and brand consistency makes them stick around."[5]

Reputation and Digital Communication

Traditionally, brand was built by companies through mass media (newspaper, radio, and the few main television channels) and was considered more about advertising and marketing than about the portrayal of the company in its entirety. Word of mouth and informal communication between customers is also not a new concept, but the medium of the Internet has changed the rate and ease by which these opinions and ideas are shared. Competitors and potential customers alike both have unprecedented access to consume and create editorial commentary, consumer reviews, news articles, and the like about both companies and individuals. Reputational risk therefore must be incorporated into all areas of risk management, including communications and customer relations. And information access can be a two-way street. Organizations can now also, faster and easier than ever, keep an eye on relevant public opinion and perception through monitoring digital sources and gathering customer feedback.

Reputational Risk

Damage caused from a reputational or branding failure can result in multifaceted and long-lasting consequences. For example, the recent security breach of EMC Corp.'s

RSA division, which resulted in the attack on defense contractor Lockheed Martin Corp., has already injured a previously stellar reputation that will likely be difficult to regain. It takes around three-and-a-half years to recover from an event resulting in reputational damage on average, though the companies with strong track records tend to recover easier.[6] Brand and reputation matters for organizations both large and small, and can be impacted both directly and indirectly by direct risks as well as risks to associates, suppliers, and partners. Reputational risk is increasingly acknowledged as a very complex part of risk management, and the most difficult to manage. Reputation can be a major competitive advantage, and a major source of disaster. Preparing for the worst and having a plan for the inevitable events that happen is part of successful reputational protection.

Johnson & Johnson: Reputation Managed Well After Crisis

The tales of poorly managed reputational incidents are numerous, but it is important to highlight the actions taken by those who have survived and overcome the risks. Johnson & Johnson's swift and decisive Tylenol recall in 1982 reveal several important factors in managing reputation in a time of crisis. After seven people died from cyanide-laced Tylenol capsules, a painkiller product responsible for 17% of the company net income the previous year, Johnson & Johnson recalled 31 million bottles. Yet the market share, which had dropped 30% after the crisis, was almost completely recovered a year later after the recall and relaunch, and the brand remains strong today.[7]

This case highlights a few particular actions that revealed how reputation can be managed even in the aftermath of a deeply damaging event.

1. Johnson & Johnson made it clear that the safety of their customers was their number one concern through the recall, which was at the time an unprecedented action. Part of a reputation is following through with action the promises that have been made.

2. The company chairman at the time, James Burke, was seen as being very upfront with the public and the media about the entire ordeal. Strong leadership and consistent communication combined with the persistent customer care helped protect the brand Johnson & Johnson had already developed. Johnson & Johnson showed they had control over the situation, and committed to fix the problem so it would never reoccur.

3. Recovering from a crisis is expensive in many ways, and still the company took the initial financial hit to fully address the problem. Over $100 million was invested after the incident,[8] with a number of follow-up campaigns in the following years. Not all organizations have the capital to spend on the scale of Johnson & Johnson, but the action of spending money on fixing the problem was a clear message to the consumer. And the financial and business results have been clear – Johnson & Johnson has been paying out increasing dividends for decades.[9]

Making Your Reputation and Brand More Resilient

There are a number of ways to work as an organization and as an individual on building a strong brand and a more resilient reputation before a crisis or incident even occurs. Taking proactive action can mitigate or even prevent some of the negative consequences that are associated with a negative failure.

1. Know your brand. Identify what the "heart & soul" of your organization is, and clearly define what that means in the practical terms you can control. Brand is not just a logotype or business collateral, but identifying how brand is manifested through those means is important to know.

2. Once you have defined it, keep the message clear and consistent. Whether it is formal communication or informal behavior, a strong reputation relies on customers and the public seeing and hearing the consistent brand of the company. Identify who is responsible for speedy and clear communication after an incident. A quick and effective response to an issue can be the most valuable pillar of keeping a strong reputation.

3. Strong leadership is key, but as Taylor mentions, brand is part of internal organizational culture as well.[10] Responsibility for organizational reputation starts at the top leadership and goes all the way down. Communicate and train employees in acceptable behavior (in both the physical and digital realms) and make sure organizational expectations are clear. For

example, an organizational social media policy that is both appropriate and understood by employees can help protect from accidental reputational damage from within.

4. Build your digital identity and increase online reputation resources. What does that mean exactly? When the inevitable incident happens an organization is going to want anyone searching online for the company to have positive search results. So before the crisis happens, proactively build your reputation. Upload and create links between organizational content, whether that means reviews, news pieces, social media sites, publications, or videos. Redundancy is often a positive feature online – you want people to be able to find things easily, and connections across the web strengthen search engine results.

Conclusion

Much of reputation risk management is as much about crisis prevention as it is about management after a crisis. Preparing and planning for the unexpected is not a simple action nor is it without cost. But the process can have significant positive returns for the organizations that invest in building their brand and making their reputations more resilient.

References

1. Fisher, Anne. "America's Most Admired Companies." *CNNMoney.com* 21 Feb. 2006: n. pag. Web. 1 Dec. 2011. <*http://money.cnn.com/2006/02/17/ news/companies/mostadmired_fortune_intro/index.htm*>

2. Tonello, Matteo. "Reputation Risk: A Corporate Governance Perspective." *Compliance Week.* The Conference Board, 2007. Web. 8 Jun 2011. <*http://*

www.complianceweek.com/s/documents/ConfBReputation.pdf>

3. Ross, Maria. *Branding Basics for Small Business: How to Create an Irresistible Brand on Any Budget.* Bedford, IN: NorlightsPress.com, 2010. Print. p. 8.

4. Taylor, Bill. "Brand Is Culture, Culture is Brand." *Harvard Business Review* n. pag. 27 Sep. 2010. Web. 09 Jun 2011. *<http://blogs.hbr.org/taylor/2010/09/brand_is_culture_culture_is_br.html>*

5. Ross, p. 25.

6. Tonello, n. pag.

7. Rehak, Judith. "Tylenol Made a Hero of Johnson & Johnson : The Recall that Started them All." *The New York Times* 23 Mar. 2002: n. pag. Web. 08 Jun 2011. *<http://www.udel.edu/richard/cisc355/Readings/tylenol.html>*

8. Rehak, n. pag.

9. Rehak, n. pag.

10. Taylor, n. pag.

Chapter II

Business Preparedness

I've written two longer pieces on pandemic planning[1] but expanded in this note past the financial sector to five additional critical infrastructure sectors in ASA's consulting practice – energy, technology, communications, public health and emergency planning. At the time this was written, most companies did not have pandemic plans in place, and if they did, they were designed to deal with the H5N1 virus, not the H1N1 virus that presented itself in the spring of 2009. I wanted the checklist provided here to be simple enough for any organization, large or small, to implement, no matter which type of flu.

Pandemic is a Predictable Surprise

Annie Searle
November 2009

We're noticing a level of boredom, sometimes tinged with sarcasm, about the appearance of the H1N1 virus, with characterizations of over-reaction by the government and the media.

In a two-year-old article, Harvard Business School Professor Max H. Bazerman described what he calls "predictable surprises … occurrences that take most people by surprise despite adequate data to predict them."[2] He indicates that the 9/11 attacks fall into this category, as does the levee breach in New Orleans, or impacts now being felt from global warming. Ironically, he had in 2007 identified both pandemic as well as "companies ignoring their financial obligations" as other looming predictable surprises.[3]

This past spring, some companies were able to rehearse their pandemic plan as the H1N1 virus spread across this and other countries. Though the spring outbreak was significant and the federal government's response was proactive, most businesses in this country still do not have the requisite policies on absenteeism and on paying employees in place.[4]

What is necessary for our leaders to pay attention to the H1N1 virus, given the amount of data now available? Bazerman notes that "our society is not good at investing now for an unclear benefit later" and goes on to say that "people are generally blamed for their actions but are not held accountable for inaction."[5]

Executives of companies who are part of our nation's critical infrastructure should begin to ensure that their companies are prepared this winter to operate at a different level if large numbers of employees are absent because of the flu:

- Identification of critical operations to maintain
- Identification of operations that would be suspended
- Splitting and segregating staff and offices
- Expanded telecommuting and teleconferencing
- Long-distance travel limits
- Local transportation issues
- Security issues
- Testing
- Education
- Communications
- Phased implementation plans
- Coordination with and among emergency-management agencies and the public-health departments

- Coordination with critical service providers and key suppliers[6]

From this general list, it becomes clear that there are complicated administrative and budget issues that must be addressed rapidly, given the volume of data that we have right now.

References

1. Searle, Annie. "US financial services sector prepares for pandemic flu," *Journal of Business Continuity and Emergency Planning*, Volume 1, Number 3, 2007, pp. 1-10; and "Pandemic readiness in the US financial services sector: When failure is not an option," *Journal of Business Continuity and Emergency Planning*, Volume 2, Number 4, 2008, pp.357-364.

2. Bazerman, Max H. "Predictable Surprises: Blind Spots in Pandemic Planning." Business Preparedness for Pandemic Conference Report, *Harvard Health Publications* Boston, MA. 2007. p. 30-31

3. Bazerman, p. 30

4. "Most Employers Lack Pandemic-Focused Comp and Absence Policies." *HR.BLR.com.* 1 June. 2009. Web. 2 June, 2009. <*http://hr.blr.com/news.aspx?id=80032*>

5. Bazerman, p. 30.

6. Excerpted from the Financial Services Sector Coordinating Council for Critical Infrastructure Protection and Homeland Security "Statement on Avian Flu Preparations," Jan. 2006.

Bhagwatwar's note chronicles the outbreak of H1N1 flu from the spring of 2009 forward. Of especial note is the last observation on how few citizens availed themselves of the no cost flu vaccine that was manufactured – certainly one of those statistics that should be inducted into the Risk Ignorance Hall of Fame. In my column that month, I noted that "...since we managed well enough through two cycles of H1N1 flu, we assume the risk is gone and that no additional precautions are necessary. It's worth re-considering those forms of complacency as we move further into the 21st century."

Handling a Pandemic

Akshay Bhagwatwar
February 2010

In the year 2009, countries around the world experienced an outbreak of a flu pandemic due to a new strain of the H1N1 influenza virus. The outbreak which was reported to have originated in Mexico rapidly spread throughout the world affecting millions of people. Many government and health authorities in different parts of the world tried to control the spread of the virus by closing down cities and the public and private facilities within the cities. The United States, Brazil, India, China and Mexico were the most affected nations with the highest number of reported cases of hospitalizations and deaths among all other countries.[1] It is challenging for health authorities to estimate the number of affected people because many people with the flu don't seek medical care and only a small number of those who seek medical are actually tested for the virus. The World Health Organization and the Centers for Disease Control and Prevention (CDC) in the United States have estimated that the number of unreported cases have crossed 100 million.[2]

The health organizations in the United States took numerous measures to prevent the spread of the virus in public places like schools, universities and other workplaces. The U.S. Department of Health and Human Services (HHS) and the Centers for Disease Control and Prevention (CDC) with the help of the U.S. Department of Homeland Security developed an updated guidance plan which the employers could use to develop or review their own prevention plans. The focus of the guidance plan was to make sure that employers are protecting people who are at a risk of getting affected by influenza related complications, maintaining their business operations and minimizing the adverse effects on their entities in the supply chain. It was apparent that the organizations across the country would have to manage their operations with a reduced workforce due to either the employees or their family members falling ill. The CDC and HHS urged the organizations that they should ask their employees to stay at home even if the organization has to face any operational issues due to reduced workforce.

Due to the concern that the virus disproportionately affects people between the age of 6 and 24, numerous schools in different countries declared temporary closures as a precautionary measure. In the United States alone, more than 600 schools were temporarily closed affecting 126,000 students in 19 states.[3] In August 2009, CDC recommended that rather than closure, schools and universities should allow students to stay home for either 7 days total or until

24 hours after symptoms subside - whichever is longer. CDC also urged schools and universities to suspend any rules related to penalizing grades based on attendance. CDC also came up with a detailed guidance plan for the universities which could be used to create awareness about the spread of the virus on campuses. CDC and HHS also made an active use of social media websites like Facebook to create awareness about the disease among youths. Social media was also used as a tool to caution public about any spam myths in circulations about the disease.

Many universities in the United States and abroad launched Pandemic Flu Prevention Strategies with the focus on creating awareness about the flu and responding urgently to flu cases on campus. The State University of New York, for example, came up with a 'Three Pronged approach to Pandemic Flu.'[4] The three critical aspects of this approach were – Prepare, Educate and Respond.[5] These aspects included several measures like launching a webpage to post all the flu related news and events, creating a university wide planning group to provide system-wide guidance on critical issues pertaining to the flu, developing tools to integrate information collected from various sources, developing channels to communicate flu related information to the state health authorities, creating points of distribution for the vaccine and so on.[6]

The measures taken by the University of Washington were on the same lines. The UW Hall Health Center also implemented several channels for creating flu awareness and distribution points for the vaccine. The Hall Health Center also developed a Flu Surveillance tool to get a count of the number of flu cases on campus. A Flu Symptoms

Self-Assessment was also developed for people who were not sure if they should visit a doctor for their flu-like symptoms.[7] Through campus wide emails and posters, universities also made sure that the updates related to the flu vaccines reached the students and staff. The vaccines were made available on university campuses at special discounted rates so that everyone could afford it. All these measures which were geared towards ensuring a control on the spread of the virus on campus were based on the guidelines suggested by the CDC and HHS.

The flu vaccine which was available starting November 2009 has been in heavy demand across the world. There have been shortages of the vaccines in several places even though the pharmaceutical companies have started the vaccine production at a rate of 3 billion doses per year. Even though the health authorities are making efforts to ensure the vaccine availability, many people have already assumed the pandemic to be over and are not taking the doses. As per a report by New York Times, by the end of January 2010, only about a fifth of Americans had taken some form of vaccine.[8] Only 40% of children and teenagers had taken the vaccine even though they are most vulnerable to infection.[9] Michael T. Osterholm, the Director for the Center for Infectious Disease Research and Policy at the University of Minnesota said in a media report that the number of people taking vaccine will increase as there might be a third wave in late February.[10] Health authorities are urging people to take the doses through various media channels to ensure that the flu does not spread much in case there is third cycle of the flu.

Reference

1. "2009 Flu Pandemic." *Wikipedia.com.* n.d. Web. Feb. 2010 *<http://en.wikipedia.org/wiki/2009_flu_pandemic>*

2. "Updated CDC Estimates of 2009 H1N1 Influenza Cases, Hospitalizations and Deaths in the United States, April 2009 – April 10, 2010. *cdc.gov.* 14 May 2010. Web. Feb. 2010. *<http://www.cdc.gov/h1n1flu/estimates_2009_h1n1.htm>*

3. "Swine Flu Closes More Than 600 Schools in U.S." *msnbc.com.* 28 Oct. 2009. Web. Feb. 2010. *<http://www.msnbc.msn.com/id/33520744#.TxXsQKVST-4>*

4. Henahan, David. "SUNY Launches H1N1 Pandemic Flu Strategy." *Suny.edu.* 14 Oct. 2009. Web. Feb. 2010. *<http://www.suny.edu/sunyNews/News.cfm?filname=2009-10-14%20Final%20SUNY%20and%20H1N1-%20Prepare,%20Educate,%20Respond.htm>*

5. Henahan, n. pag.

6. Henahan, n. pag.

7. "H1N1 Influenza." *Depts.washington.edu.* University of Washington. n. d. Web. Feb. 2010. *<http://depts.washington.edu/hhpccweb/h1n1/wp/>*

8. McNeil, Donald, Jr. "Most Americans Think Swine Flu Pandemic is Over, a Harvard Poll Finds." *New York Times.* 5 Feb. 2010. Web. Feb. 2010. *<http://www.nytimes.com/2010/02/06/health/06flu.html>*

9. Donald, n. pag.

10. Donald, n. pag.

It is very difficult to obtain useful data about the costs of disasters and recovery efforts, but Munshi has done a good job here of looking globally and researching any reports on costs that are available. His report was written shortly after both Haiti and Chile had experienced major earthquakes

Data on Disasters: Before and After

Shirish Munshi
March 2010

Introduction

While making a risk management plan, disasters like earthquakes, flooding etc. play a pivotal role. The natural events can wipe out development gains and accumulated wealth in developed as well as developing countries. The cost of disasters both in terms of lost Gross Domestic Product (GDP), as well as spending or relief and rehabilitation is significant.

In March 2004, the World Bank released a report on the costs associated with the natural disasters. Natural disasters lead to monetary loss as well as human lives. From 1990 to 2000, the number of people affected by natural disaster tripled to 2 billion.[1] These statistics are crucial to analyze the difference between costs of mitigating the loss caused by such disasters and the costs of spending after the disasters occur. In this research note, we have explained the costs associated with the natural disasters that occurred and later part of the document contains the costs associated in mitigating the loss caused by such disasters.

Disaster Data

According to the Center for Research on the Epidemiology of Disasters (CRED), 326 natural disasters and 259 technological disasters were reported worldwide in 2008.[2] Out of the total costs of US$ 181 billion, Hurricane Katrina caused maximum damage amounting to almost US$ 140 billion (2008 prices). Nine of the fifteen natural disasters with damages equal to or superior to US$ 1 billion occurred in North America and two in Europe; of the four that occurred in Asia, three hit China.[3] The table on page 38 shows the total amount of disaster estimated damages (by continent) from 1999-2008 in million US$.

9/11 Terrorists Attack

The September 11, 2001 terrorists attack can be counted as an unexpected catastrophic disaster that caused loss of millions of dollars. The below data gives an estimate about costs associated with the September 11 attack.

Economic loss to New York in month following the attacks: $105 billion

Estimated cost of cleanup: $600 million

Total FEMA money spent on the emergency: $970 million

Estimated amount donated to 9/11 charities: $1.4 billion

Estimated amount of insurance paid worldwide related to 9/11: $40.2 billion

Estimated amount of money needed to overhaul lower- Manhattan subways: $7.5 billion

Amount of money recently granted by U.S. government to overhaul lower-Manhattan subways: $4.55 billion

Estimated amount of money raised for funds dedicated to NYPD and FDNY families: $500 million.[4]

Total amount of disaster estimated damage, by continent and by year (1999 to 2008) in millions of US$ (2008 prices)

	1999	2000	2001	2002	2003	2004	2005	2006	2007	2008	Total
Africa	802	1,248	808	438	6,480	1,915	38	244	784	341	13,097
Americas	28,602	6,672	16,006	15,446	25,357	74,301	190,499	7,251	18,293	61,983	444,411
Asia	44,427	27,204	15,743	15,914	27,734	75,600	30,603	24,961	35,874	115,935	413,995
Europe	65,714	22,254	2,403	40,431	21,496	2,079	17,323	2,594	22,393	2,803	199,489
Oceania	2,899	670	698	2,610	694	630	241	1,373	1,493	90	11,399
High human development¹	89,092	41,473	19,768	63,700	54,088	127,943	207,866	13,281	57,069	64,128	738,409
Medium human development	53,325	8,523	15,822	11,078	27,670	25,980	30,825	23,139	21,280	117,023	334,666
Low human development	25	8,052	68	60	3	602	13	3	489	n.a.	9,316
Total	142,443	58,048	35,658	74,838	81,761	154,525	238,704	36,424	78,838	181,152	1,082,391

Source: EM-DAT, CRED, University of Louvain, Belgium

¹ See note on UNDP's Human Development Index country status in the section on disaster definitions in the introduction to this annex.
Note: n.a. signifies no data available. For more information, see section on caveats in introductory text.

As mentioned in the introduction, damage assessment is frequently unreliable. Even for existing data, the methodologies are not standardized and the financial coverage can vary significantly. Depending on where the disaster occurred and who reports it, estimations may vary from zero to billions of US dollars.

The total amount of damage (US$ 181 billion) reported in 2008 is the second highest of the decade and is largely above the decade's average (US$ 108 billion), but still below the peak of 2005 (US$ 239 billion).

In 2008, in Asia, reported disaster damages were the highest of the decade, accounting for 64 per cent of all damages reported in the world. The Sichuan earthquake alone accounts for 45 per cent of all reported damages.

For the second time in the decade, in 2008 damage in medium human development countries was greater than that reported for high human development countries.

5

Hurricane Katrina

The 2005 hurricane season was unprecedented in its scope and magnitude. More than three million insurance claims totaling some $57 billion resulted from four hurricanes-Katrina, Wilma, Rita and Dennis. Katrina generated the largest single loss in the history of insurance – $40.6 billion and more than 1.7 million claims – across six states – Louisiana, Mississippi, Alabama, Florida, Tennessee, and Georgia.[6]

Chile Earthquake 2010

AIR Worldwide catastrophe risk modeling firm estimated that the insured loss from the quake will exceed $2 billion.[7] That estimate came from Boston-based AIR Worldwide, which said the economic losses may exceed $15 billion or 7,875 billion Chilean pesos.[8] The death toll from the earthquake currently exceeds 700. The company said this equates to 10-to-15 percent of Chile's real GDP.[9]

Disaster Risks Prevention

Is it possible to prevent natural disasters? Many people argue on the fact that vulnerability to natural hazards is so obvious then why do we even bother to think about disaster risks and preventive measures and trends in the occurrence of such risks? The main concern in preventing disaster risks is early warning and early action. It is high time to unite and to take concrete concerted actions, for securing human life and livelihoods and protecting socio-economic gains and opportunities.

Natural Calamity Prevention by DREF

According to World Disasters Report 2009, the International Federation Disaster Relief Emergency Fund (DREF) provides rapid funds for emergency preparedness and disaster response.[10] For example, in 2007, emergency preparedness helped DREF to save many lives from hurricane in Guinea.[11] Since 2004, the use of DREF has grown from 4.7 million to 17.8 million in 2008. The graph below shows DREF operations and costs in small-scale emergencies and large scale emergencies from 2004 to 2008.

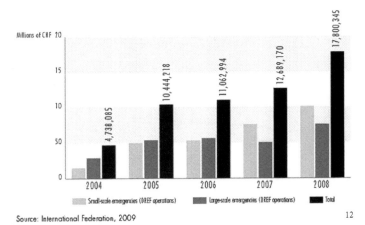

Source: International Federation, 2009   12

The distribution chart on the next page gives the types of operations of DREF in different natural disasters. The majority of operations were carried out for floods and cyclones.

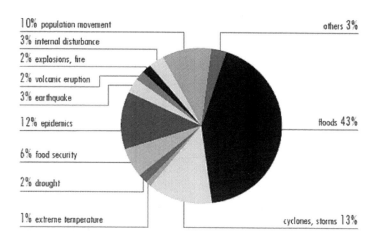

10% population movement

3% internal disturbance

2% explosions, fire

2% volcanic eruption

3% earthquake

12% epidemics

6% food security

2% drought

1% extreme temperature

others 3%

floods 43%

cyclones, storms 13%

Source: International Federation, 2009   13

Cyber Security Prevention Expenditure

In 2009, the Pentagon spent $100 million in a period of six months for cyber defense.[14] The number included the cost of housing and feeding technicians as well as the cost of training technicians to handle new threats. "Each compromised machine, costs the Pentagon $5,000 to $7,000, without counting the price of people."[15]

In the private sector, the cost of data breaches is recognized to be high, but few cases cost $100 million. "The most recent annual survey released in February 2009 by the Ponemon Institute on the cost of a data breach in 2008 concluded that breaches cost about $200 per record. The survey covered breaches ranging in size from 4,200 records to over 113,000 records, so a breach compromising 113,000 records would cost, according to this data, over $22 million."[16]

Terrorism Prevention by Department of Homeland Security (DHS)

DHS has made considerable progress in strengthening the security of commercial aviation and seaports since September 11, 2001, and increased its focus on securing surface modes of transportation, including mass transit. From fiscal years 2006 to 2008, DHS has allocated about $755 million dollars to transit agencies through its Transit Security Grant Program to protect transit systems and the public from terrorist attacks.[17]

Early Action Pays

There are good analyses of the benefits of investment in risk mitigation. For instance, the cost of adjustments in the design of a deep water port in Dominica would have cost only 28 percent of the repair costs after it was damaged by a tropical storm, as stated by U.S. Agency for International Development and Organization of American State.[18]

For the United States, according to the U.S. Multi-Hazard Mitigation Council: "On average, a dollar spent by FEMA (US Federal Emergency Management Agency) on hazard mitigation provides the nation with about $4 in future benefits."[19] In addition, "FEMA grants to mitigate the effects of floods, hurricanes, tornados and earthquakes between 1993 and 2003 would save more than 220 lives and prevent almost 4,700 injuries over approximately 50 years."[20]

These results of investing into risk mitigation not only worked in bigger countries like United States, but also in small countries. For instance, small-scale mitigation works in Nepal (building of check dams to prevent erosion and save land and crops), carried out by the Nepal Red Cross with support of British Red Cross, provided a benefit-cost ratio of 18.6.[21]

The traditional response of waiting for the emergency to occur and then flying tablets from much further away, not only take longer, but also results in high transportation costs.[22] As an example, in 2008 West Africa flood response by Red Cross Societies, which was supported by a regional preparedness appeal based on a seasonal forecast, suggest that the combined cost of preparedness and response per beneficiary was about a third lower than the costs of response alone in 2007, the previous heavy flood season.[23]

Miscellaneous data

- The Institute of Business and Home Safety quoted – "About 25% of the companies do not reopen following a major disaster."[24]

- A government study says the cost of flood damage could rise from about £1bn a year to £20bn by 2080 in the most extreme scenario.[25]

- The table on the next page shows the probability of occurrence of different natural disasters.

Phenomenon and direction of trend	Likelihood of future trend based on projections for the 21st century
Warm spells/heatwaves – frequency increase	Very likely*
Heavy precipitation events – frequency increase, or proportion of total rainfall from heavy falls increase	Very likely
Area affected by drought – increase	Likely
Intense tropical cyclone activity – increase	Likely
Extreme high sea level (includes tsunamis) – incidence increase	Likely

Source: Adapted from IPCC, 2007

*Very likely = >90% probability of occurrence, according to expert judgement. Likely = >66% probability of occurrence.

References

1. "Natural Disasters: Counting the Cost." *WorldBank.org.* 2 Mar. 2004. Web. Mar. 2010. <*http://web.worldbank.org/WBSITE/EXTERNAL/NE WS/0,,contentMDK:20169861~pagePK:64257043~piPK:437376~theSi tePK:4607,00.html*>

2. "World Disaster Report 2009." *International Federation of Red Cross and Red Crescent Societies.* Geneva, Switzerland, 2009. Web. Mar. 2010. <*http://www.ifrc.org/Global/WDR2009-full.pdf*>

3. World Disaster Report, 155.

4. "The Encyclopedia of 9/11." *New York Mag.* n.d. Web. Mar. 2010. <*http://nymag.com/news/articles/wtc/*>

5. World Disaster Report, p. 165.

6. "Impact on U.S. Small Business of Natural and Manmade Disasters." *Hewlett Packard and SCORE.* 2007. Web. Mar. 2010. n. pag. <*http://www.webwizebackup.com/impactofDisaster.pdf*>

7. Hays, Daniel. "Chile Insured Loss Will Exceed $2 Billion, Modeler Estimates." *Propertycasualty360.com.* 1 Mar. 2010. Web. Mar. 2010 <*http://www.propertycasualty360.com/2010/03/01/chile-economic-damage-could-hit-30-billion-modeler-estimates*>

8. Hays, n. pag.

9. Hays, n. pag.

10. World Disaster Report.

11. World Disaster Report, p. 77.

12. World Disaster Report, p. 77.

13. World Disaster Report, p. 78.

14. Goldman, Alex. "Pentagon Claims $100M in Cybersecurity Costs." *Internetnews.com.* 8 April. 2009. Web. Mar. 2010.<*http://www.internetnews.com/government/article.php/3814461/Pentagon+Claims+100M+in+Cybersecurity+Costs.htm*>

15. Goldman, n. pag.

16. Goldman, n. pag.

17. "Transit Security Grant Program." *goa.gov.* June 2009. n. pag. Web. Mar. 2010. <*http://www.gao.gov/new.items/d09491.pdf*>

18. World Disaster Report, p. 88.

19. "Natural Hazard Mitigation Saves." *National Institute of Building Sciences, Mutltihazard Mitigation Council.* 2005. p. iii. Web. Mar. 2010. *<http://www.nibs.org/client/assets/files/mmc/Part1_final.pdf>*

20. Natural Hazard, p. iii.

21. World Disaster Report, p. 89.

22. World Disaster Report, p. 89.

23. World Disaster Report, p. 89.

24. Impact on Small, n. pag.

25. "'Holistic' Approach to Flood Plain Build." *Bbcnew.com.* 22 April. 2004. Web. Mar. 2010. *<http://news.bbc.co.uk/2/hi/uk_news/3649663.stm>*

26. World Disaster Report, p. 100.

Some research notes are written to provide basic and foundational information on risk themes. In the spring of 2010, Bhagwatwar wrote this basic research article to coincide with "Disaster Preparedness Month" in the United States.

Disaster Preparedness

By Akshay Bhagwatwar
April 2010

Disaster management is the discipline that includes preparing for disasters before they occur, disaster response and supporting the recovery phase after the disaster.[1] Nations around the world lose billions of dollars due to the natural and technological disasters as well as terrorism.[2] Multinational companies also invest money in preparing their disaster management plans with an aim of ensuring business continuity. The focus of all these disaster preparedness or emergency management activities is on reducing the economic and social impact of the disaster as well as on ensuring a speedy recovery and rebuilding process. Being prepared for a disaster can reduce fear, anxiety and losses that might happen. Local government and many disaster-relief organizations always run to help individuals and organizations when disasters happen. However, there are situations where such organizations may not be able to reach the affected place immediately. It is such situations where having your own disaster management plan will help in reducing the damages.

According to a 2010 report by FEMA, disaster preparedness can be viewed as a four phased method comprising of mitigation, preparedness, response and recovery.[3]

4

The mitigation phase focuses on implementation of long term measures for reducing or eliminating risks. Thus, the focus during this phase is on ensuing that possible hazards do not turn out to be total disasters. The preparedness phase is where the risk managers or the emergency managers develop an action plan in preparation for the possible disasters. The action plan commonly has measures developing communication plans, stockpiling and maintaining disaster supplies, building and training emergency response teams, developing emergency evacuation plans and so on. The disaster phase generally consists of the Disaster Relief Operation. This includes the dispatch of the core emergency services like the firefighters, police and ambulance crew. They may be supported by a large number of secondary emergency services such as emergency rescue teams. The recovery phase is focused on restoring or rebuilding the affected properties, repairing the critical infrastructure and re-employment. It is critical for the emergency managers to put an effort on ensuring the continuity of operations even when the recovery phase is in operation.

Many Government agencies like the Federal Emergency Management Agency (FEMA) release disaster preparedness checklists and kits to help individuals, communities and organizations prepare their disaster preparedness plan. FEMA has the 'Are You Ready? An in-depth Guide to Citizen Preparedness' accessible publicly on their website.[5] The guide provides a step-by-step approach to disaster preparedness by walking the reader through how to get informed about local emergency plans, how to identify hazards that affect their local area, and how to develop and maintain an emergency communications plan and disaster supplies kit.[6] The guide also covers evacuation, emergency public shelters, animals in disaster, and information specific to people with disabilities.[7] The FEMA also developed the HAZUS (Hazards United States) software package which is central in the risk assessment process in the country.[8] The current version of the HAZUS software is capable of modeling three types of hazards: flooding, hurricanes, and earthquakes.[9] HAZUS has also been adopted by emergency management organizations worldwide.[10]

The month of April brings in the theme of disaster preparedness in the United States. The Washington State's Emergency Management Division published the 'In-Focus 2010' webpage recently with a special focus on earthquake preparedness activities.[11] The division has also published checklists, questionnaires and videos for individuals, groups, schools and businesses to help them with their disaster management plans. In addition to resources for natural disaster management planning, the division has also published H1N1 guidance webpage focused on helping schools with their H1N1 avoidance and response planning.[12] An example of a successful disaster preparedness program in the Washington State is the Puget Sound Regional Catastrophic Preparedness Planning Program (RCPP) which was created in 2008 to enhance regional catastrophic preparedness. The scenarios for the Puget Sound RCPP are two: (1) Catastrophic earthquake – likely a shallow-crust earthquake along the Seattle Fault and (2) A mass–aerosolized attack in the downtown Seattle core. The RCPP covers eight counties in the Puget Sound Area. It has three central objectives: to address shortcomings in the existing plans; to building regional planning processes and communities; and to link operational and capabilities-based planning with resource allocation.[13] The details of the RCPP plan are available on the City of Seattle website.[14]

Business Continuity and disaster preparedness are one of the six ASA focus areas that ASA offers services in. ASA also published a research note in March which contains data related to various disasters in the United States as well as in other nations. The research note can be accessed on the ASA website's Research Notes section.

References

1. "Emergency Mangement." *Wikipedia.com.* n. d. April 2010. Web. <*http://en.wikipedia.org/wiki/Disaster_preparedness*>

2. "Are We Ready?" *The Council for Excellence in Government.* 14 Dec. 2006. Web. April 2010. <*http://www.citizencorps.gov/downloads/pdf/ready/pri_report.pdf*>

3. "Developing and Maintaining Emergency Operations Plans." *Federal Emergency Management Agency.* p. 18. Nov. 2010. Web. Jan. 2012. <*http://www.fema.gov/pdf/about/divisions/npd/CPG_101_V2.pdf*>

4. Image adapted from <*http://www.fema.gov/pdf/about/divisions/npd/CPG_101_V2.pdf*>

5. "Are You Ready? Guide." *Ready.gov. Federal Emergency Management Agency.* n. d. n. pag. Web. April 2010. <*http://www.ready.gov/are-you-ready-guide*>

6. "Are You Ready?" n. pag.

7. "Are You Ready?" n. pag.

8. "HAZUS." *Federal Emergency Management Agency.* n. d. Web. April 2010. <*http://www.fema.gov/plan/prevent/hazus/index.shtm*>

9. "HAZUS," n. pag.

10. "HAZUS," n. pag.

11. "Washington Disaster Preparedness Month." *emd.wa.gov.* April 2010. Web. April 2010. <*http://www.emd.wa.gov/preparedness/prep_infocus_WADisasterPrepMonth.shtml*>

12. "H1N1 (Swine Flu) Guidance." *emd.wa.gov.* n.d. Web. April 2010. <*http://www.emd.wa.gov/preparedness/prep_swineflu.shtml*>

13. "Puget Sound Regional Catastrophic Preparedness Program." *Seattle. gov.* 16 Sept. 2008. Web. April 2010 <*http://www.seattle.gov/emergency/library/Attachment%20A.%20PUGET%20SOUND%20RCPP%20EXEC%20SUMMARY.pdf*>

14. "Puget Sound Regional," n. pag.

Bhagwatwar's note is one of the more in depth studies of the Gulf Oil Spill, consolidating all available intelligence at the time it was written. Clearly British Petroleum underestimated the risk of such a spill and ignored data that was available from significant prior oil spills, including the Montara spill in 2009. Since this was written, we also know that regulators had not performed regular inspections, and that contingency plans were weak at best, with little or no testing of the plans that existed. This research note, together with the one that follows by Shirish Munshi, provide valuable analysis of the event itself.

The Gulf Oil Spill of 2010

Akshay Bhagwatwar
June 2010

The Gulf oil spill of 2010 started with the catastrophic explosion and subsequent fire on the Deepwater Horizon offshore oil drilling platform situated about 40 miles southeast of the Louisiana coast. The explosion killed 11 platform workers while 17 others were injured. This resulted into the sinking of the Deepwater Horizon and resulted into the start of the largest oil spill in U.S. history.[1] More than just an oil spill, it is also known to be a great environmental disaster.

Analysis of Risks and the Precautions Taken Prior to the Explosion

Drilling rigs are huge and complex mechanical machines which have to operate under adverse weather conditions where possibility of human errors is high. The records of Mineral Management Service (a branch of the U.S. Department of the Interior that oversees offshore drilling) show that there have been 39 incidences of fires or explosion in the Gulf in the first half of 2009.[2] The number is an astonishing 858 if the fires and explosions since 2001 are taken into consideration. BP had filed a 52 page exploration and environmental impact plan with the Mineral Management Service in 2008.[3] BP's plan stated that it was "unlikely that an accidental surface or subsurface oil spill would occur from the proposed activities."[4] The plan stated that even if an accident takes place, it would have no adverse impacts since the well was situated 48 miles away from the shore and the implemented response capabilities were very effective.[5] The Department of the Interior exempted BP's Gulf of Mexico drilling operation from a detailed environmental impact study after concluding that a massive oil spill was unlikely.[6] In addition, following a loosening of regulations in 2008, BP was not required to file a detailed blowout plan.[7]

The Rig Explosion and the Oil Spill

The fire aboard the Deepwater Horizon started on the night of April 20, 2010. The interviews with platform workers conducted as part of BP's internal investigation revealed that the event was basically a blowout. A bubble of methane gas escaped from the well and shot up the drill column, expanding quickly as it burst through several seals and barriers before exploding.[8] According to officials, 126 individuals were on board, of whom 79 were Transocean employees, six were from BP, and 41 were contracted. Of these, 115 individuals were evacuated and 11 other were reported to be dead.[9]

On the afternoon of April 22, 2010, a large oil slick began to spread at the former rig site.[10] BP initially estimated that the wellhead was leaking 1,000 barrels (42,000 U.S. gallons) a day.[11] However, this estimate was later revised by BP at 12,000 to 100,000 barrels (500,000 to 4,200,000 U.S. gallons) per day.[12] The exact spill flow rate is uncertain because BP has refused to allow independent scientists to perform accurate measurements. The resulting oil slick covers a surface area of at least 6,800 km^2, with the exact size and location of the slick fluctuating from day to day depending on weather conditions.[13] BP has started working on different short and long term methods to stop the oil spill. However, none of the attempts till now have succeeded. Experts fear that the spill will result in an extensive impact on the marine and wildlife habitats in the region. The spill has also damaged the Gulf of Mexico fishing and tourism industries.

Questionable Risk Management Practices

Many experts consider the oil spill of 2010 to be remarkably similar to what happened during the 1979 Ixtoc I explosion and the subsequent oil spill. Even the measures taken in 1979 are similar to what is being done to stop the 2010 oil spill. The 1979 oil spill which lasted for more than 10 months (3 June 1979 – 23 March 1980) had resulted into a loss of 3 million barrels of oil and oil spread of 2800 km2.[14] The methods tried to stop the oil spill in 1979 were also similar to what is being tried for the 2010 oil spill. Even in 1979, the dome method was tried and it had failed horribly. This is the prime reason why the use of dome method again for the 2010 oil spill is being questioned by experts. The thing that helped stop the spill in 1979 was the drilling of relief wells which took several months for implementation.[15]

The oil industry's technological advancement and the lessons learnt from previous oil spills are questionable. It is not really necessary to compare the oil spill with something that happened 30 years back. Less than a year ago, there was a catastrophic oil spill, known as the Montara Oil Spill in the Timor Sea (between Indonesia and Australia). In that oil spill, a Thai company's well blew out in a similar fashion. The amount of oil wasted in the Montara Oil Spill is estimated anywhere between 1.2 to 9 million gallons. Similar methods to stop oil spill were tried and had failed drastically. It took ten weeks and a total of five attempts at drilling relief well to stop the Montara oil spill.[16]

The oil spill has definitely exposed the inadequacy of BP's disaster prevention processes and contingency planning. "The only thing that's clear is that there was a catastrophic failure of risk management," said Nansen Saleri, a Houston-based expert in oil-reservoir management.[17] Oil industry experts have also questioned why it took the company so long to come up with possible solutions, and why it didn't have possible solutions to use in hand. "There should be technology that's pre-existing and ready to deploy at the drop of a hat. It shouldn't have to be designed and fabricated now, from scratch," said one former Transocean executive.[18] BP's general spill plan, which was updated in summer of 2009, indicates that BP's claimed abilities to handle a spill were overestimated. BP had stated in the plan that the worst spill from a mobile drilling operation would come from a lease called the Mississippi Canyon 462, about 33 miles off the Louisiana coast.[19] A blowout of that lease could discharge 250,000 barrels a day which is 50 times the estimated flow of the current leak.[20] Yet BP claimed to have sufficient equipment in place to deal with a spill far in excess of the volume it is struggling to handle.[21]

BP's executives and media spokesmen have been defending the actions. BP spokesman Andrew Gowers said, "The unthinkable has become thinkable, and the whole industry will be asking searching questions of itself. We moved very rapidly to implement the approved response to the accident. The evidence for that is the huge containment effort on the surface and onshore."[22] It added: "There were multiple control mechanisms, procedures and equipment in place that should have prevented this accident or reduced the impact of the spill.[23] These did not succeed.

The Deepwater Horizon disaster may or may not have been preventable, but a better contingency plan surely should have been in place to deal with the disaster. It also seems that if all the "what if" questions had been asked prior to the explosion, speedier answers to the problems would have been available. As BP continues to work on stopping the oil spill, it has pledged $500 million for an "open" investigation into the spill, and to research better ways of tracking oil spills with technology.

References

1. Zeller, Tom, Jr. "Estimates Suggest Spill is Biggest in U.S. History." *New York Times.* 27 May 2010. Web June 2010. <*http://www.nytimes.com/2010/05/28/us/28flow.html*>

2. Grant, G. "Gulf of Mexico Oil Spill was no Accident." *Powellriversersuader.blogspot.com.* 12 June 2010. Web. June 2010. <*http://powellriverpersuader.blogspot.com/2010/06/gulf-of-mexico-oil-spill-was-no.html*>

3. Grant, n. pag.

4. Burdeau, Cain and Holbrook Mohr. "BP Didn't Plan for Major Spill." *adn.com.* 1 May 2010. Web. June 2010. *<http://www.adn. com/2010/05/01/1258669/bp-didnt-plan-for-major-spill.html>*

5. Burdeau, Holbrook, n. pag.

6. Burdeau, Holbrook, n. pag.

7. Burdeau, Holbrook, n. pag.

8. "BP Probe: Blowout Triggered by Methane Gas." *cbsnews.com.* 8 May 2010. Web. June 2010. *<http://www.cbsnews.com/stories/2010/05/07/ national/main6468952.shtml>*

9. "Deepwater Horizon Oil Spill." *Wikipedia.com.* n.d. Web. June 2010. *<http://en.wikipedia.org/wiki/Deepwater_Horizon_oil_spill>*

10. Farid, Mike. "Gulf Oil Spill in Pictures and Videos." *Astromic.blogspot. com.* 11 June 2010. Web. June 2010. *<http://astromic.blogspot. com/2010/06/gulf-oil-spill-in-pictures-and-videos.html>*

11. Wikipedia, n. pag.

12. Wikipedia, n. pag.

13. Gibbons, David. "The Gulf of Mexico Disaster." *Davidgibbons.org.* 10 June 2010. Web. June 2010. *<http://www.davidgibbons.org/id311.html>*

14. "Oil Spill." *Wikipedia.com.* n.d. Web. June 2010. *<http://en.wikipedia. org/wiki/Oil_spill>*

15. Cook, Tracy Lynn. "BP – Worst Oil Spill – Repeat of Ixtoc 1979, Gulf of Mexico." *gather.com.* 27 May 2010. Web. *<http://news.gather.com/ viewArticle.action?articleId=281474978263199>*

16. Tercek, Mark. "The Oil Spill and the Controversy's Response." *Cool Green Science.* 1 May 2010. Web. June 2010. *<http://blog.nature. org/2010/05/mark-tercek-gulf-oil-spill-nature-conservancy/>*

17. Chazan, Guy, and Neil King. "BP's Preparedness for Major Crisis is Questioned." *The Wall Street Journal.* 10 May 2010. Web. June 2010. *<http://online.wsj.com/article/SB1000142405274870430780457523462 1987007784.html>*

18. Chazan, n. pag.

19. Chazan, n. pag.

20. Chazan, n. pag.

21. Chazan, n. pag.

22. Chazan, n. pag.

23. King, Leo. "BP Oil Spill 'Slows' but Serious IT Failures Come to Surface." *Cio.com.* 28 May 2010. Web. June 2010. <*http://www.cio.com/ article/595620/BP_Oil_Spill_Slows_but_Serious_IT_Failures_Come_ to_Surface*>

Munshi's note covers a lot of ground, including the fact that a similar spill had taken place with the Ixtoc I blowout in 1979; and detail on what happens with such a disaster converges with a natural disaster in events such as the Exxon Valdez spill with the Gulf of Alaska storm in 1989. What is clear is that history repeats itself – especially if a second disaster is added to the first.

Hurricanes and Oil Spills

Shirish Munshi
July 2010

Introduction

The Deepwater Horizon Spill (also known as BP Spill, the Gulf of Mexico Spill) is a massive ongoing oil spill in the Gulf of Mexico that is the largest offshore spill in U.S. history. This spill has an extensive environmental impact already apparent on the marine and wildlife habitats. As the hurricane season is here, and the Deepwater Horizon Spill is still discharging a geyser of oil into the Gulf of Mexico, we anticipate a hurricane agitating through the largest accidental oil spill in history.[1]

Possible Effects of Hurricane on Gulf Oil Spill

There are lots of unknowns about what could be the possible effect of a hurricane on the natural ecosystem. The closest call came in 1979, after the greatest accidental oil spill in history, the massive Ixtoc I blowout. "That catastrophe dumped 3 million barrels (126 million gallons) of oil into the Southern Gulf of Mexico between June 1979 and March 1980."[2] Category 1 Hurricane Henri passed just north of the main portion of the oil spill on September 16 and 17, generating 15 foot seas and southwest winds of 15 - 25 knots over the spill region on the 16th."[3]

Interestingly, the NOAA/AOML report on the spill found that "the winds did not blow long enough or strongly enough to control the direction of oil flow, as evidenced by the fact that the wind direction was often 180° to the direction of plume flow. The main impact of the wind was to dilute the oil and weather it, converting it to a thick "mousse."[4] James H. Cowan, a biological oceanographer at Louisiana State University, said a hurricane could push oil inland, possibly affecting rice and sugar cane crops.[5] A hurricane could also delay attempts to close the well and could spread/dilute the oil further or deeper in the ocean.[6]

Jeff Masters, founder of Weather Underground, pointed out the possibility of more widespread damage to coastal areas, airborne oil droplets immersed in hurricane winds, and a chance that the oil spill could cause explosive deepening of hurricanes in the Gulf.[7]

"Larry Crowder, a professor of marine biology at Duke University, said that if the spill continues for a couple more months, then oil almost certainly would get into the Loop Current that flows clockwise around the Gulf. It then would be a week to 10 days before it got to the Florida Keys, and a couple of weeks more before the Gulf Stream carried it to North Carolina."[8]

NOAA's position is that the oil spill would have a "minimal" effect on a hurricane's behavior, as long as the spill is small in comparison to the storm. Also, "the high winds and rough seas would aid in the weathering process of the oil slick, and the agency discarded the possibility of petroleum being embedded in the hurricane's precipitation. However, NOAA stressed that the direction of any spreading of oil due to the passage of a tropical cyclone depends on the exact track of the storm, and cautioned that the hurricane's storm surge may carry oil inland. Hurricanes also could disperse the oil farther and wider - or roil the waters so that oil at the surface plunges to great depths and poisons the deep water ecosystem."[9]

Recently, the hurricane Alex, with winds of 85 mph, was headed for the northeastern Mexico and South Texas coasts late on Wednesday, June 30, according to the National Hurricane Center. That is far from the oil spill site off the coast of Louisiana.[10]

Shores that are already fouled by oil will probably benefit from a hurricane, but the oil cleaned off of those shores then becomes someone else's problem. "The strong winds and powerful ocean currents that a hurricane's winds drive will bring oil to large stretches of coast that otherwise would not have gotten oil. This is the major concern regarding a hurricane moving through the Deepwater Horizon oil spill."[11] Let's consider the case of the Exxon Valdez disaster in 1989. "The ill-fated tanker split open in Prince William Sound on March 24, and oil spill response crews were initially able to contain the spill behind booms and make good progress removing it. However, two days later, a powerful Gulf of Alaska storm with 70 mph winds roared through, overwhelming the containment booms and distributing the oil along a 90-mile stretch of coast. The oil went on to foul over 400 miles of Alaska coast, a far larger disaster than would have occurred than if the storm had not passed by."[12] Similarly, a hurricane moving through the Gulf of Mexico spill will very likely make the disaster much worse, spreading out the oil over a larger region, and bringing the oil to shores that otherwise might not have seen oil. It is true that the oil will be diluted some by being spread out over a larger area, so some shores will not see a substantial oiling. But overall, a hurricane passing through the oil spill is likely to result in much higher damage to the coast. "Similarly, Katrina's storm surge destroyed an oil tank at Chevron's Empire facility, releasing oil into a retention pond in a region surrounded by marshland. Three and half weeks later, Hurricane Rita's storm surge hit the oily mess in the retention pond, washing 4,000 - 8,000 gallons of oil into nearby marshlands, which were heavily or moderately oiled."[13] The oiled marshlands were set on fire six weeks after the spill, resulting in 80-90% removal of the oil and contaminated vegetation.[14] The marshland recovered fairly quickly, though oil still remained in the roots, affecting burrowing crabs and the wildlife that feed on them. So, oiled marshes can recover somewhat from a storm-surge driven oiling, but it is uncertain if burning could be successfully used to restore a 100+ square mile region of marshland oiled by the storm surge from a major hurricane.[15]

Therefore, the Deepwater Oil Spill already had severe consequences for BP. To add to it, the occurrence of a hurricane would create havoc for BP, U.S. Government and cause a threat to natural ecosystem.

References

1. Avery, Heidi. "The Ongoing Administration-Wide Response to the Deepwater BP Oil Spill." *The White House Blog*. 5 May 2010. Web. 15 July 2010. <*http://www.whitehouse.gov/blog/2010/05/05/ongoing-administration-wide-response-deepwater-bp-oil-spill*>

2. Masters, Jeff. "What Would a Hurricane do to the Deepwater Horizon Oil Spill?" *wunderground.com*. 26 May 2010. Web. 15 July. 2010. <*http://www.wunderground.com/blog/JeffMasters/comment.html?entrynum=1492*>

3. Master, n. pag.

4. Master, n. pag.

5. "British Petroleum = Jinx." *British Petroluem Jinx*. n.d. Web. July 2010. <*http://britishpetroleumjinx.unblog.fr/2010/07/30/bonjour-tout-le-monde/*>

6. Master, n. pag.

7. Master, n. pag.

8. Schoof, Renee, and Chris Adams. "Top Kill's Failure Means Gulf Oil Spill Will Only get Worse." 30 May 2010. Web. July 2010. <*http://www.mcclatchydc.com/2010/05/30/95075/gulf-oil-spill-this-disaster-just.html*>

9. Schoof, n. pag.

10. "Hurricane Alex Wind Speeds now 85 MPH or 135 KM/HR." *FromTheOld.com*. 30 June 2010. Web. July 2010. <*http://fromtheold.com/news/alex-wind-speeds-now-85-mph-or-135-kmhr-2010063018763.html*>

11. Masters, n. pag.

12. Masters, n. pag.

13. Masters, n. pag.

14. Masters, n. pag.

15. Masters, n. pag.

Munshi prepared this note to coincide with National Preparedness Month in September of 2010. In my column for that month, I noted that "Today's work climate is fraught with anxiety and peril. Operations run leaner than ever before, often without redundant safeguards. Critical core processes are outsourced or off-shored to save money. We know that there are cracks in the business infrastructure. Programs to handle business continuity, security, audits and compliance are highly leveraged. A range of threats can hurt the reputation and brand of the company, large or small." The threat of an earthquake is certainly one of the largest threats that certain parts of this country face.

Earthquake Preparedness

Shirish Munshi
September 2010

Introduction

One of the most frightening and destructive phenomena of nature is a severe earthquake and its terrible after-effects. An earthquake is a sudden movement of the earth, caused by the abrupt release of strain that has accumulated over a long time. If the earthquake occurs in a populated area, it may cause many deaths and injuries and extensive property damage. It's important for a business to be prepared for a disaster like an earthquake. Moreover, the business should be capable of recovering quickly from an earthquake with least amount of losses. This research note discusses few simple steps to have an earthquake resilient business.

Are you prepared?

Being prepared can reduce human and monetary losses that accompany disasters for a business. Business should be ready to evacuate their employees and help them take refuge in public shelters and know how to care for their basic medical needs. This can only be done if the business has a continuity and emergency plan and follow the below mentioned steps:

1. Identify Risks and Capabilities: The foremost step is to identify what may interrupt your business operations temporarily or worse. It is important to know what kinds of emergencies might affect your company both internally and externally. Businesses should try to find out if it's an earthquake prone area and the probability of occurrence of an earthquake. For specific earthquake hazard information, "Putting Down Roots in Earthquake Country" provides excellent information on faults, earthquake forecasts, potential losses in major earthquakes, how to get prepared, and more."[1] This can also be done by performing a business impact analysis for potential emergency scenarios.

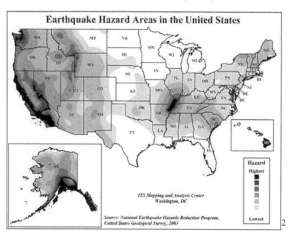

Earthquake Hazard Areas in the United States

ITS Mapping and Analysis Center
Washington, DC

Source: National Earthquake Hazards Reduction Program,
United States Geological Survey, 2003

2. Business Continuity Planning: How quickly your company can get back to business after an earthquake often depends on emergency planning developed today. Businesses should start planning now to improve the likelihood that your company will survive and recover. This can be done by carefully assessing and reviewing your company's business process flow chart. The next step is to identify the business operations that are critical for the company to survive and recovery as quickly as possible. If your business has a key supplier of resources, it might be possible that the disaster shuts down your supplier. It's important to create a list of critical business contractors and others for emergency situations. The management should include co-workers from all levels in planning and as active members of the emergency management team. It's vital to consider a broad cross-section of people from throughout your organization, but focus on those with expertise vital to daily business functions. These will likely include people with technical skills as well as managers and executives.[3] The next step is to define crisis management procedures and individual responsibilities in advance. The management should make sure those involved know what they are supposed to do. Not only this, but train others in case you need back-up help. An emergency plan should be reviewed annually as the business changes over time. When a business hires new employees or when there are changes in how your company functions, you should update your plans and inform your people.

3. Implement Structural Hazard Mitigation Plan: It is important for the business to mitigate the structural and non-structural risks to the business. This can be done by

increasing the seismic safety of the building structures and installing fire sprinklers. The IT infrastructure can be prevented from damage by using loop fasteners and hooks to servers, computers, network devices and other valuable items from falling.[4] Also, installing anchors on pallet rack frames can secure your rack system to help avoid accidents during an earthquake event.

4. Emergency Planning for Employees: Human resources are business's most important and valuable asset. There are some procedures you can put in place before a disaster, but you should also learn about what people need to recover after a disaster. "It is possible that your staff will need time to ensure the well-being of their family members, but getting back to work is important to the personal recovery of people who have experienced disasters. It is important to re-establish routines, when possible."[6] According to

FEMA, "two- way communication is central before, during and after a disaster."[7] This can be done by including emergency preparedness information in newsletters, on company intranet, periodic employee emails and other internal communications tools.[8] The business should consider setting up a telephone calling tree, an email alert or a call-in voice recording to communicate with employees in an emergency. It is also important to engage people with disabilities in emergency planning. They should be asked about communications difficulties, physical limitations, equipment instructions and medication procedures. The emergency plan should be frequently reviewed and drills and exercises must be conducted to test the plan.

5. Emergency Supplies for Employees: After an earthquake occurs, businesses will need to be self-sufficient as first responders will be addressing high priorities such as hospitals and schools. There should be trained personnel

to find and help anyone injured. The next step is to find if the building is safe to stay after damage. Moreover, it is important for the business to provide basic necessities like food, water and sanitation to their employees. Recommended emergency supplies by FEMA are:

a. Water, amounts for portable kits will vary. Individuals should determine what amount they are able to both store comfortably and to transport to other locations. If it is feasible, store one gallon of water per person per day, for drinking and sanitation

b. Food, at least a three-day supply of non-perishable food

c. Battery-powered radio and extra batteries

d. Flashlight and extra batteries

e. First Aid kit

f. Whistle to signal for help

g. Dust or filter masks, readily available in hardware stores, which are rated based on how small a particle they filter

h. Moist towelettes for sanitation

i. Wrench or pliers to turn off utilities

j. Can opener for food (if kit contains canned food)

k. Plastic sheeting and duct tape to "seal the room"

l. Garbage bags and plastic ties for personal sanitation.[10]

By following these steps, small and large organizations can reduce the impact of an earthquake and help the business to recover quickly after the earthquake is over.

References

1. "Every Business Should Have a Plan." *FEMA Ready Business*. 17 Sept. 2004. p.2. Web. 1 Sept. 2010. <*http://www.ready.gov/sites/default/files/documents/files/BusinessPlan_brochure.pdf*>

2. Image taken from <*http://anbaupm.com/Page.aspx?pageId=8*>.

3. FEMA, p. 2.

4. "7 Steps to an Earthquake Resilient Business." *Southern California Earthquake Center*. 11 April 2008. Web. 1 Sept. 2010. <*http://www.earthquakecountry.info./*>

5. Image taken from *http://www.cssyes.com/Warehouse-Earthquake-Safety-Inspection.htm*.

6. FEMA, p. 2.

7. FEMA, p. 2.

8. FEMA, p. 2.

9. Image taken from http://www.pep-c.org/howsafeisyourhome/.

10. FEMA, p. 2.

Small to mid-size businesses have had inordinate challenges in the past several years in the midst of an economic recession. Here, in an edited and revised note that had the original title of "Communicating Crisis Management Value: Understanding the Value of Preparing for Unexpected Events for Small-to-Medium Size Businesses," Oxenford examines how the value of crisis management and disaster preparedness planning can be conveyed to executives.

The Disaster Preparedness Gap

Emily Oxenford
December 2010

Introduction

Major events in the U.S. in recent years, such as the H1N1 pandemic of 2009, numerous hurricanes, cyber-attacks and extreme weather conditions have caused companies of all sizes and industries to pay more attention to preparing for the next emergency or disaster that will disrupt their business operations. Small and Medium Enterprises (SMEs) can find themselves particularly vulnerable to disasters and emergencies, and the U.S. Small Business Administration reports that an estimated 25 percent of American small businesses cannot reopen after experiencing a major disruption.[1] Any business, regardless of size, is not successful without investments of time, money and resources. Small businesses in particular require a heavy investment from owners, and therefore the investment is even higher. The stakes are higher, and the risks associated with SMEs can be more dramatic and potentially devastating. Disaster preparedness plans and programs are critical, since businesses with a program can usually better ride out a disaster. A plan can greatly assist a company to efficiently re-establish contact with employees, vendors and customers, and help the firm get back to business more quickly following a disaster.

A Gap Between Knowledge & Action

While awareness of disaster vulnerability is slowly improving among business of all sizes, the knowledge of potential harm is not necessarily being translated into action. One survey of SMEs by the Center for Catastrophe Preparedness & Response conducted in 2006 found while 85 percent of SMEs surveyed had made some kind of preparations for preparedness, only 23 percent had a formal written program in place.[2] The pattern emerges that while many SMEs acknowledge the need for disaster preparation and recovery, they often fail to invest in planning for the unexpected events that can cause serious damage or even result in going out of business. A survey conducted in the United States by research agency TNS NFO reported that 40 percent of small business respondents admitted they were unprepared for a disaster, and a third had no current plans to begin preparedness activities.[3] The survey findings also revealed that close to one in five businesses (18 percent) did not back up their data at all, and nation-wide a full 25 percent of small business owners described their attitude towards disaster preparedness as "live and let live," preferring to deal with a disaster when it occurs than prepare for potential crises.[4] Clearly a number of small and medium enterprises are facing difficulties in connecting the knowledge of disaster preparedness with the actions necessary to implement disaster preparedness actions.

The Data is Out There

The value of disaster preparedness is steadily becoming a more prominent national conversation for businesses of all sizes and industries. A wide breathe of research and studies have been published in recent years, and the information is becoming more visible in business communities. The challenge for business owners can be to connect the relevancy of the data to their own operations and risk profile.

The small and medium sized business owners surveyed in 2006 cited risk to employees and business operations (69 percent), legal liability (51 percent), reputation (49 percent), and insurance requirements (37 percent) as major motivators to prepare for disasters.[5] The survey by the Center for Catastrophe Preparedness & Response also notes that the most common reason (46 percent) businesses give for not taking steps to prepare for disaster is that they do not have enough information on how to prepare. Other reasons included the lack of financial & staff resources (41 percent), not enough expertise (32 percent), lack of a strong business case (26 percent) and not enough time (23 percent).[6] The survey results highlight the fact that businesses that see a business rationale for disaster preparedness are more likely to prepare, and that firms that do not see a clear business rationale connection are less likely to prepare.

Communication from Risk Professionals

Ultimately, the value of disaster planning has to be understood by the business owners before any action happens.

Risk professionals, both inside small businesses and those looking in, have an increasing array of tools and data to build better cases for disaster preparedness. The clear preparedness gap discussed earlier will not begin to close on its own, and risk professionals will be key players in future progress. Opportunities for risk professionals to connect with business owners are increasingly available as SMEs both observe and experience the repercussions of disasters of all types.

Risk professionals are experts at identifying risks, but also must become experts at communicating risks in ways that speak to the context of SMEs. The critical issue particularly for SMEs is that they must scale planning appropriately for their business. Communicating that planning can be done to fit a company's needs and resources are critical to starting the planning process. No business owner will get on board a preparedness project that they perceive is beyond their needs or abilities. Even after disaster preparedness planning has begun, it is critical for risk professions to involve leadership and decision makers in the process, continually providing reminders about how risk planning continues to be a valuable and worthwhile use of company resources and time. The ultimate goal of communicating risk in context is the importance of finding methods for risk to be communicated "in a way that informs without frightening, educates without provoking alarm, and moves people to act."[7]

References

1.   "Disaster Preparedness." *U.S. Small Business Administration*, n.d. Web. 11 Nov. 2010. <*http://archive.sba.gov/services/disasterassistance/ disasterpreparedness/index.html*>

2. "New York's Small and Medium Sized Businesses Are Not Prepared For Emergencies. Why?" *Center for Catastrophe Preparedness & Response, The International Center for Enterprise Preparedness, The American Red Cross in Greater New York*. 2006. Web. 07 Nov. 2010. <*http://www.nyu.edu/ccpr/NYC-Business-Preparedness-FINAL-BR.pdf*>

3. "Survey: 40 Percent of Small Businesses Have No Disaster Preparedness Plan." *Contingency Planning and Management* (2008). Web. 15 Nov. 2010. <*http://contingencyplanning.com/articles/2008/06/04/survey-40-percent-of-small-businesses-have-no-disaster-preparedness-plan.aspx*>

4. *Contingency Planning & Management*, n. pag.

5. *CCPR, ICEP, ARC*, 2006.

6. *CCPR, ICEP, ARC,* 2006.

7. Tinker, Tim L., and Gerald E. Galloway, Jr. "How to Communicate Flood Risks Effectively." *Journal of Business Continuity & Emergency Planning* 3, no. 3 (2009): 193.

Here Oxenford sets out to examine why there is no global archive of lessons learned from natural disasters that is accessible to emergency managers in both the public and private sector. She attributes the absence of such an archive to the complexity of the events, the lack of management decision-making, and gaps in information. Without such a compendium, we are working on each new disaster with one hand metaphorically tied behind our backs. Worse still, the gaps in disaster response never get addressed.

Lessons Learned – Where Are They?

Emily Oxenford
April 2011

Facing Global Disasters

The devastation of environmental disasters can be epic – ranging from the damage to individual lives, to the communities and their businesses, all the way up to governments and the devastation of entire regions. In just the last few years, the world has witnessed catastrophic events that have ravaged populations, economies, and infrastructures. A few of the most prominent disasters have been:

- Indian Ocean Tsunami (2004)
- Hurricane Katrina (2005)
- Pakistan Earthquake (2005)
- Deepwater Horizon Oil Spill (2010)
- Eyjafjallajökull Volcanic Eruptions (2010)
- Haitian Earthquake (2010)

- Japanese Earthquake (2011)

Following disasters of this scale, it is normal for scholars, practitioners, and communities to reflect on the preventative measures, responses, and recovery steps surrounding the disaster. As time goes on, more knowledge is often gathered or generated about how to better handle disasters in the future. Regardless of sector or field, governments, businesses, health organizations, emergency responders, and individuals all have something to learn from the experiences during previous disasters. But these lessons learned often are not integrated into standards and best practices. The lessons that are being listed now from the 2011 earthquake in Japan do not seem to be different than those already in existence, built from the experiences with previous earthquakes.

Where are the Lessons?

The reasons behind low-levels of incorporation seem to be because of 1) the complexity of large-scale disasters 2) the lack of high-level decision-making and enforcement and 3) the gaps and barriers in information flow between all parties.

The complexity makes lessons learned both difficult to document and tricky to apply across sectors and needs. The lessons for local governments preparing for disaster, for example, might appear to be quite different from those of humanitarian organizations arriving at a disaster zone bringing aid. A local government is going to have to deal with the politics of legislators and taxpayers, for example, who may not approve the funds to cover in-depth disaster planning. This might be especially difficult if the community has not suffered a disaster for a period of time, and public interest is low.

The lack of decision makers and power to enforce decisions is particularly tricky for large-scale disasters. The problems with organizing relief and charity organizations in a disaster environment have been both identified and discussed, but there are still very few implemented best practices for how to solve the coordination and logistics issues. This is closely related to the troubles of information flow.

The flow of information surrounding lessons learned seems to be quite stunted across various channels. Regardless of level, there is a lack of sharing and collaboration when it comes to building lessons learned. Governments often do not share with other governments, businesses keep disaster plans internal because of security concerns, scholars publish to limited academic journals, and grass-roots efforts are sometimes never seen beyond the communities they are grown from. Regardless of why, the lessons learned are not reaching many of the organizations and people that they could.

Ewing and Synolakis[1] cite Jonientz-Trisler et al.,[2] who identified five factors for resilience when it comes to disasters, which emerged out of research about the 2004 Indian Ocean tsunami. These five characteristics identify how to increase resilience in the face of disaster.

1.   Understand the nature of the hazard

2.   Have the tools needed to mitigate the risk

3.   Disseminate information about the hazard

4. Exchange information with other at-risk areas

5. Institutionalize planning for a disaster

To reach a robust level of resilience, these elements require cooperation beyond an individual level. They also sum up the importance of an integration of lessons learned. Each step requires knowledge about how previous disasters have been handled, and the identification of information flows.

Creating a Risk Framework

The goal of documenting and implementing lessons learned is to develop standards and good practice, regardless of industry. One of the struggles in integrating lessons learned, building on the three factors earlier identified, is the lack of a risk framework.

For example, Bob Weinhold[3] notes one area that lacks the implementation of lessons learned is the health standards and protection for emergency responders. Local, national, and international teams make up the emergency and disaster responders, and depending on the location and disaster, there are limited standards for how to best protect the people who put themselves on the line to help the victims of disasters. Budgets often dictate what procedures are followed, sometimes just the bare minimums rather than established best practices. From the approach of mitigating future risks (often health related), the lessons of the past need to be integrated into the standards for emergency responders.

The question of who is in charge of enforcing and regulating the implementation of lessons learned is a key one. Especially during large-scale environmental disasters such as the Deepwater Horizon oil spill and the Japanese earthquake, there are many different players and the problems of politics and jurisdiction must be taken into account. The issues of risk can be more easily addressed within such a complicated environment if there is a clear framework to approach disasters. The recent efforts of FEMA to integrate Public-Private Partnership models is one step in the right direction for creating cross-sector frameworks for approaching the risks in disaster preparation and response. And computer scientists like Schurr et al.[4] are exploring new ways for computer software to capture lessons from disasters and then use those lessons to better equip first responders with useful tools to help them. Collaboration and communication are keys to creating better standards that take the lessons of disasters and build the future plans upon them.

Conclusion

Unfortunately, it seems that the multi-dimensional nature of environmental disasters leaves many organizations and individuals feeling overwhelmed. The lack of lessons learned being part of future practical disaster management is a critical gap in the approach towards coping with the inevitable disasters that will strike. Businesses, governments, and individuals must strive to not only capture and document the lessons to be learned from disasters, but also work to find practical ways to implement and integrate lessons into standards and practices.

References

1.   Ewing, Lesley C., Costas E. Synolakis. "Community Resilience: Lessons from Recent Disasters." Proceedings of the International Conference on Coastal Engineering, 2010; 32.

2.   Jonientz-Trisler, C., Simmons, R. S., Yanagi, B. S., Crawford, G. L., Darienzo, M., Eisner, R. K., Petty, E., and Priest, G. R. "Planning for Tsunami-Resilient Communities." *Natural Hazards*, 2010; 35, 121–139

3.   Weinhold, Bob. "Emergency Responder Health: What Have We Learned from Past Disasters?" *Environmental Health Perspectives*. August 2010; 118(8): A346-A350. Web. April 2011.*<http://www.ncbi. nlm.nih.gov/pmc/articles/PMC2920106/>*

4.   Schurr, Nathan, Janusz Marecki, Paul Scerri, J. P. Lewis, Milind Tambe, "The DEFACTO System: Training Tool for Incident Commanders" *The Seventeenth Innovative Applications of Artificial Intelligence Conference (IAAI)* 2005. Web. April 2010. *<http://teamcore.usc.edu/papers/2005/ IAAI052SchurrN.pdf>*

Over the past five or so years, we've seen FEMA in action, working with local officials at the site of our country's largest disasters and in follow up recovery efforts. Certainly FEMA has evolved over time, particularly in the past five years. It is a leader in using social media tools and explicitly looks to citizens to participate in its programs. Here Hansen explains the background behind the formation of FEMA as well as the Stafford Act of 1988.

Recovering With FEMA

Andrew H. R. Hansen
September 2011

Introduction

The last half-century has been witness to natural and man-inflicted disasters which have left potentially crippling effects in their wake. With the primary aim of helping people prepare for and recover from disaster, the United States Federal Government created the Federal Emergency Management Agency (FEMA). By reviewing a brief history of major legislation and gaining understanding of how FEMA can help companies and individuals today, organizations can better prepare themselves to manage the unexpected.

Brief History

Overview by Decade 1930-1950

1930s

- Congress establishes the Reconstruction Finance Corporation, which had authority to grant loans to states in response to emergency

- Bureau of Public Roads given authority to provide financial relief to rebuild highways and bridges damaged by natural disasters

- National Flood Program created; establishing Federal responsibility to assist flood mitigation programs along major rivers

1940s

- Civil defense established to protect civilians

1950s

- Disaster Relief Act of 1950 gives presidential authority to declare disaster areas which authorizes federal agencies to provide direct support to state and local governments

- Federal Civil Defense Act of 1950 created a nation-wide system of civil defense agencies

The earliest piece of federal legislation aimed at disaster recovery assistance can be traced all the way back to the Congressional Act of 1803.[1] Following a series of devastating fires in New Hampshire, this act brought relief to local merchants by waiving duties and tariffs on imported goods.[2] Over the next several decades, "ad hoc legislation was passed more than 100 times in response to hurricanes, earthquakes, and other disasters."[3] But by the 1930s, "when the federal approach to problems"[4] was gaining traction, new, more comprehensive legislation was beginning to take shape.

Throughout 1960s-1970s, the United States was hit with a series of major hurricanes and earthquakes. Helping assist in recovery from these natural disasters, over "100 different federal agencies were collectively involved in the relief efforts."[5] This involvement of so many government[6] organizations often resulted with internal bickering about authority, and led people to "complain about the lack of coordination and poor results."[7] The Disaster Relief Act of 1974 attempted to address some of these concerns, but following continued pressure by state governors, President Jimmy Carter created the Federal Emergency Management Agency (FEMA) in April of 1979.[8]

For many years FEMA operated as an independent government agency, largely able to respond effectively to natural disasters and weather the differences brought about by changing administrations. In 1988, the Robert T. Stafford Disaster Relief and Emergency Assistance Act (Stafford Act) amended the Disaster Relief Act of 1974 in an effort to further streamline and clarify federal assistance in natural disaster responses.

Following the terrorist attacks of 2001, Congress passed the Homeland Security Act of 2002, which resulted in the creation of the Department of Homeland Security in 2003. At this time FEMA was "downgraded from an independent agency to a sub-department of Homeland Security,"[9] where it remains today.

How FEMA Works

FEMA's mission is to "support our citizens and first responders to ensure that as a nation we work together to build, sustain, and improve our capability to prepare for, protect against, respond to, recover from, and mitigate hazards."[10] The Stafford Act of 1988 helped shape the response framework used by FEMA today. Awareness of how FEMA works and an understanding of the types of available assistance can help individuals and companies be prepared to respond to the unpredictable.

Following the occurrence of a disaster, and a State declaration of emergency, "the State will evaluate the recovery capabilities of the State and local governments. If it is determined that the damage is beyond their recovery capability, the governor will normally send a request letter to the President… The president then makes the decision whether or not to declare a major disaster an emergency."[11] An emergency declared by the President, "triggers financial and physical assistance through the FEMA."[12]

The Stafford Act also laid the ground work for the Public Assistance Grant Program. This program reimburses eligible entities for approved "expenses they incurred in protecting lives and property ahead of storms, and in cleaning up and rebuilding afterward."[13] The grant program also helps by rebuilding "infrastructure that is better able to withstand future storms."[14]

Assistance to Governments

There are four major entity types that are eligible for public grant funds:

1. State government agencies, such as:

    - Departments of transportation
    - Environmental resources agencies
    - State parks agencies
    - Water quality commissions

2. Local governments, including:

- Towns, cities, parishes
- Municipalities, townships
- Local public authorities

3. Private nonprofit organizations or institutions that are open to the public and that provide certain services otherwise performed by a government agency. Eligible facilities are limited to:

- Educational
- Emergency
- Medical
- Utilities
- Custodial care
- Irrigation organizations
- Other essential government services.[15]

4. Federally recognized Indian tribes or authorized organizations and Native village organizations[16]

Assistance to Individuals

In addition to providing assistance to governments, FEMA provides a number of services geared towards individuals. They include:

Disaster Assistance: Provides money or direct assistance to individuals, families and businesses in an area whose property has been damaged or destroyed and whose losses are not covered by insurance

Crisis Counseling: Provides supplemental funding to States for short-term crisis counseling services to people affected in Presidentially declared disasters

Disaster Legal Services: Provides free legal assistance to disaster victims

Disaster Unemployment Assistance Program: Provides unemployment benefits and re-employment services to individuals who have become unemployed because of major disasters

National Flood Insurance Program: Enables property owners in participating communities to purchase insurance as a protection against flood losses in exchange for State and community floodplain management regulations that reduce future flood damages.[17]

Current Organization

FEMA is organized into ten regional offices, with headquarters in Washington, D.C. As of September 10, 2011, FEMA has 7,559 employees located across the country.[18] 2011 has been a record breaking year with FEMA offices responding to 222 disaster declarations, a 41 percent increase over the previous record from 1996.[19] Response to this unusually high number of disasters has resulted in spending at a pace of $30 to $40 million per day.[20]

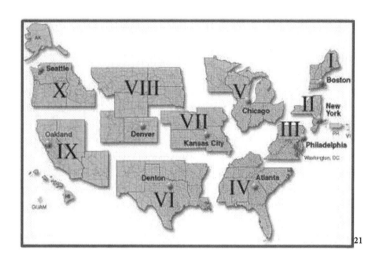

21

Conclusion

From simple, sporadic legislative beginnings, FEMA has progressively attempted to streamline their efforts to better prepare and more comprehensively serve American citizens. Because it is a publically funded organization, FEMA will always be subject to the objectives of changing administrations; but the primary goals of FEMA will likely remain consistent. Businesses and individuals should be aware of the ways FEMA can assist them in order to expedite recovery efforts and return to normal operation.

References

1.   "Emergency Management History." *Phillipsburgnj.org.* n.d. Web. 7 Oct. 2011. *<http://www.phillipsburgnj.org/pdf/ACF4A8.pdf>*

2.   Salter, Jim. "FEMA Puts Long-Term Rebuilding on Hold After Irene." *Yahoo.finance.com.* Associated Press. 30 Aug. 2011. Web. 7 Oct. 2011. *<http://finance.yahoo.com/news/FEMA-puts-longterm-rebuilding-apf-1314272650.html>*

3.   "Emergency Management History," n. pag.

4.   "Emergency Management History," n. pag.

5.   "A Short History of FEMA." *Pbs.com.* n.d. n. pag. Web. 7 Oct. 2011.
     <http://www.pbs.org/wgbh/pages/frontline/storm/etc/femahist.html>

6.   Image adapted from *http://www.phillipsburgnj.org/pdf/ACF4A8.pdf.*

7.   "A Short History," n. pag.

8.   "A Short History," n. pag.

9.   "A Short History," n. pag.

10. "About FEMA." *Fema.gov.* n.d. n. pag. Web. 8 Oct. 2011. *<http://www.
     fema.gov/about/index.shtm>*

11. "Presidential Disaster Declaration" *Fema.gov.* Web. 8 Oct. 2011. *<http://
     www.fema.gov/government/grant/pa/pr_declaration.shtm>*

12. "Presidential Disaster," n. pag.

13. "FEMA Public Assistance Program Helps Oklahoma Rebuild Roads,
     Repair Power Lines, and More." Fema.gov. n. pag. 22 Mar. 2010. Web.
     8 Oct. 2011. *<http://www.fema.gov/news/newsrelease.fema?id=50647>*

14. "FEMA Public Assistance," n. pag.

15. "Infrastructure Projects." *Fema.gov.* n.d. Web. 8 Oct. 2011. *<http://
     www.fema.gov/plan/ehp/noma/projects2.shtm>*

16. "Infrastructure Projects," n. pag.

17. "Grants and Assistance Programs for Individuals." *Fema.gov.* n.d. Web.
     8 Oct. 2011. *<http://www.fema.gov/individual/grant.shtm>*

18. "About FEMA," n. pag.

19. Mayer, Matt. "Federal Budget Makes Case That FEMA Reforms are
     Needed." *The Heritage Foundation.* 28 Sept. 2011. Web. 8 Oct. 2011.
     *<http://www.heritage.org/research/reports/2011/09/federal-budget-
     makes-case-fema-reforms-needed>*

20. Mayer, n. pag.

21. Image taken from *http://www.fema.gov/about/contact/regions.shtm.*

CHAPTER III

BUSINESS SECURITY

Where the line is drawn between privacy and security has been a focus of attention for ASA research since 2009. Especially in the banking and finance sector, with the advent of the Patriot Act in 2001 (to fight terrorism) and the Bank Secrecy Act in 1970 (to fight money-laundering), the amount of monitoring and reporting of individual transactions has increased significantly in the name of counter-terrorism. Here Oxenford discusses a proposed set of financial reporting rules affecting cross border transactions which would add more overhead to the reporting that the financial sector already performs. This particular proposed regulation received significant pushback from the well-organized banking and financial sector and has, as a result, stalled out.

The Proposed FinCEN Reporting Regulations: Privacy, Security and the Cross-border Electronic Transmittals of Funds

Emily Oxenford
October 2010

Introduction

Recently, on the 27th of September 2010, the Financial Crimes Enforcement Network (FinCEN) released a new set of rules that would change the way banks and other financial institutions record and report any money transfers in and out across the U.S. border. Referred to as cross-border electronic transmittals of funds (CBETF), these new requirements, if passed by the U.S. Department of Treasury, would compel banks to report every international transaction, regardless of monetary amount or suspicious behavior. Additionally, each bank would be required to give an annual report including the taxpayer identification number of everyone who had either sent or received a CBETF.

Background

In the press release given by FinCEN, the Intelligence Reform and Terrorism Prevention Act (IRTPA) is cited as the source of the requirements that the new proposal would fulfill.[1]

The basis of these laws, though, goes back to 1995. At that time, FinCEN issued a policy that required "banks and nonbank financial institutions to collect and retain information on certain funds transfers and transmittals of funds" and to also "include certain information on funds transfers and transmittals of funds to other banks or nonbank financial institutions."[2] These rules were created in order to better aid law enforcement agencies and those required to regulate financial systems to "detect, investigate, and prosecute money laundering and other financial crimes by preserving an information trail about persons sending and receiving funds through the funds transfer system."[3] The newest set of regulations builds on this precedence, and integrates the results from the 9/11 Commission report.

New Proposal

The new rules proposed by FinCEN, if approved by the Department of Treasury, would set new reporting standards for various financial institutions that deal with international monetary transactions. Banks would be required to report to FinCEN every CBETF processed through their institution, whether received or sent and regardless of amount. Money services businesses (MSBs) would also be required to report any CBETFs that they process equal to or greater than $1,000 USD. As mentioned previously, banks would also be required to report the taxpayer identification numbers.[4]

Justification

The new laws grew from a stipulation in the IRTPA for FinCEN to analyze the feasibility of these kinds of reporting requirements, "if the Secretary determines that reporting of such transmittals is reasonably necessary to conduct the efforts of the Secretary against money laundering and terrorist financing."[5] Conducting that feasibility analysis, FinCEN reports that these new laws would be possible, and that they could help law enforcement officers better identify and stop transnational criminal activity, whether organized crime, drug cartels, terrorism, or tax-evasion.[6] FinCEN's press release claims that the new laws would be possible, given that "current regulations already require that these financial institutions maintain and make available, but not affirmatively report, essentially the same CBETF information."[7] Allowing a centralized database to be created of these kinds of transaction would enable swifter and more accurate investigations into potential security threats.

The Feasibility Report conducted by FinCEN regarding the implementation of these new policies concluded that the data they want to collect is "reasonably necessary to support the Secretary's efforts to combat money laundering and terrorist financing. Specifically, the inability to conduct proactive analysis on the information currently recorded by banks hinders law enforcement's ability to identify significant relationships to active targets."[8]

One argument that is made by the FinCEN report as well is that at the time, the existing reporting requirements for electronic funds transfers "were not sufficient to alert law enforcement agencies to the more than $130,000 sent to the 19 9/11 hijackers via electronic funds transfers."[9] Of course, tracking financial transaction is only one of the many sources of complex data law enforcement agencies must sift through.

Privacy versus Security

Benjamin Franklin has been attributed with variations of the quote "Those who desire to give up freedom in order to gain security will not have, nor do they deserve, either one." There is sometimes a very fine line between security and privacy – it should be carefully considered what privacy in financial transactions is given up to potentially identify security threats. Perhaps the most important question that arises from these regulations is whether or not the invasion of privacy is worth any additional security that is gained from these rules. The purpose of banking regulations is truly to create and sustain a safe and secure system for financial transactions. Is it the role of the banks and MSBs to become an extension of the law enforcement agency, at the expense of their customers' privacy? Or are they responsible for providing the information in order to protect the "bigger" picture of their customers' security?

Conclusion

If these new rules do pass, individuals, financial institutions, and non-financial organizations will all have to integrate awareness about where their financial information is being shared into their everyday practices.

Other alternatives to reporting all CBETFs and tax-payer identification numbers should also be considered. One of the arguments by FinCEN itself is the importance of having data available and centrally located – but there is much more than financial data that needs to be central-ized and made available. One of the biggest difficulties our law enforcement communities face is the segregation and decentralization of various bits of data that could make up a more complete picture of the security landscape.

References

1. Hudak, Steve. "FinCEN Proposes Regulatory Requirement for Financial Institution to Report Cross-Border Electronic Transmittals of Funds." *Financial Crimes Enforcement Network*, 27 Sept. 2010. Web. 8 Oct. 2010. *http://www.fincen.gov/news_room/nr/pdf/20100927.pdf*

2. Financial Crimes Enforcement Network; Cross-border Electronic Transmittal of Funds. *Department of Treasury, Cryptome.org.* Federal Register. 75.189: p. 60377-60397. Web. 11 Oct. 2011. *<http://cryptome.org/0002/fincen093010.htm>*

3. Hudak, n. pag.

4. Sandord, Travis. "FinCEN Wants to Know." *Courthouse News Service.* 1 Oct. 2010. Web. 11 Oct. 2010. *<http://www.courthousenews.com/>*

5. Hudak, n. pag.

6. Hudak, n. pag.

7. Hudak, n. pag.

8. Financial Crimes Enforcement, n.pag.

9. Sanford, n.pag.

Data has been a focus of ASA's Institute of Research and Innovation since its inception in 2009. Data breaches have increased significantly since that time, both in the public and private sector. In the private sector, such losses can challenge customer retention programs as the costs to make the customer whole become a significant issue on the balance sheet. Oxenford explores the issues in detail, then provides a high level checklist that companies can use to review the effectiveness of their internal controls.

Data Loss and Business Responsibility

Emily Oxenford
March 2011

Introduction

The vast amounts of data being created, edited, stored, transported, and analyzed on a daily basis is astronomical. For businesses, more and more critical services and products are driven by and completely dependent on data. With a growing quantity of data and expanding risks to data, a business must be increasingly protective of data, ensuring that neither business operations nor customer data are compromised.

But many businesses are not addressing the issue of data loss, a risk that could not only severely damage a business but could even close it down for good. A study done a few years ago found that nearly half of IT and compliance professionals said that "their organizations are doing an inadequate job of lowering the rate of data loss" and that they would be unable to notify users and customers of a data breach.[1] From the same research study, it was found that most of the 1,000+ people surveyed felt that their organizations did not possess "the necessary security tools or internal controls to prevent, detect, and correct data security breaches."[2] This is a serious problem that highlights the need for businesses to consider the serious problem that data loss represents.

Responsibility

In order to account for responsibility, it is important for a business to determine to whom they are responsible. For the purposes of this discussion, this research will assume an obligation of responsibilities to employees, customers, community, and shareholders. These four groups are all part of making or breaking the success of a business, and therefore there is an obligation towards them from an organization's perspective.

A business has an obligation to protect its customer data from things such as loss, fraud, and theft.[3] An organization may also be said to owe its customers and stakeholders clear communication about the status and use of data. In certain sectors, such as finance, there are legal obligations that require communication to customers when data has been lost or compromised. But in sectors where there are little or no legal obligations for compliance, it is often left to the business to self-regulate. This self-regulation certainly benefits a business in general (poorly handled data will likely result in loss of reputation, finances, and business), but it is sometimes tricky to implement full preventative measures without the government or legal incentives. There are many decisions to be balanced in a business - the protection of data should be incorporated into both policy and practice to ensure priority.[4]

Data Loss

There are three trends[5] that have been identified as reasons for why data loss is a rising issue among businesses, even though there is also an increasing awareness about the critical nature of protecting an organization's data.

There is an increased storage capacity for data in fewer devices and for less money. This means that while businesses can afford to store more and more, the repercussions of that storage being compromised are significantly higher.

There are so many types of information that are being recorded and stored in digital formats. In the information age, we see that data has become key to business operations and services. The loss of this data can have devastating results on a business, and either cripple or kill the future of a company.

The ability to backup and recover data is increasing, but the tools and methods are not always perfect. People sometimes rely too heavily on the software or hardware to ensure the complete, frequent, and healthy (non-corrupted) backup of data.

It is important to understand how data loss can occur. According to research done by the Protect-Data.com,[6] there are five main causes for both an organization and individual to experience data-loss.

Hardware or System Malfunctions (44%)
- Electrical failure
- Head/media

- Controller failure

Human Error (32%)
- Accidental deletion
- Accidental drive format
- Damage by drop or fall

Software Corruption (14%)
- Corruption caused by diagnostic or repair tools
- Failed backups
- Configuration complexit

Computer Viruses (7%)
- Boot sector viruses
- File infecting viruses
- Polymorphic viruses

Natural Disasters (3%)
- Fires
- Floods
- Brownouts/Lightning Strikes
- High Wind

These different causes are not comprehensive, but certainly represent many of the different threat sources a business must consider when preparing for the increasingly common risk of data loss.

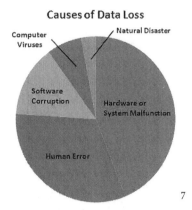

Causes of Data Loss

Prevention Measures

There are a number of steps to ensure that data is protected, both during day-to-day operations and during a disaster or crisis. Adapting these measures to fit the business context and needs should be considered an important part of any risk planning.

Technical Safeguards

A number of important recommendations for the protection of data come from the PCI DSS (Payment Card Industry Data Security Standard),[8] which deal with the protection of data in the credit-card industry. These are not limited to this particular industry, and in fact can be adapted into any business where data is created, edited, and moved. A challenge for many businesses is limited financial and personnel resources to dedicate to the implementation of preventive safeguards, but the investment can result in a significant payoff if disaster does strike.

- Install and maintain a firewall configuration to protect data
- Do not use vendor-supplied defaults for system passwords and other security parameters
- Protect stored data
- Encrypt transmission of data and sensitive information across public networks
- Use and regularly update anti-virus software
- Develop and maintain secure systems and applications
- Restrict access to data by business need-to-know
- Assign a unique ID to each person with computer access
- Restrict physical access to data
- Track and monitor all access to network resources and data
- Regularly test security systems and processes
- Maintain a policy that addresses information security policy.[9]

Business-Practice Safeguards

It is not sufficient to implement technical safeguards and assume that the system will be enough to protect data. Planning for risk as a whole needs to be part of business culture and practice. As part of risk management, the following safeguards can help address not only data loss, but help in other risk areas within a business.

- Internal company review of policies, procedures and controls. Knowing the existing state of these is one of the first steps of identifying and closing gaps in a business.

- Third-party review of policies, procedures and controls. An outside perspective is often necessary for painting a complete picture, but ownership and responsibility is not transferred.

- Identify standards that third-party vendors must meet. The risk of data-loss is not limited to internal practices, and communicating with partners and vendors can be key to mitigating risk.

- Company-wide awareness and training program. This is important for making risk planning and prevention part of business culture and practice.[10]

Conclusion

Keeping in mind the increasingly critical nature of data to businesses and their customers, it is equally as important to prioritize the protection of said data. Businesses need to not only protect data but in the event of its loss, take up the responsibility to recover, restore, and replace it as they are able as part of their responsibility to stakeholders. Strong prevention is key, though, in reducing the threat of data loss in the first place.

References

1.   Gaudin, Sharon. "IT Managers Say Risk of Data Loss Is Bad and Getting Worse." *InformationWeek*.com 18 June 2007. Mar. 2011. <*http://www. informationweek.com/news/199905013*>

2.   Gaudin, n. pag.

3.   Leppik, Peter. "To Whom Does an Ethical Business Owe a Responsibility." *Blog Dispatches from the Frozen North.* 24 Feb 2004. Web. Mar. 2011. <*http://www.frozennorth.org/C1848698620/ E2013508927/index.html*>

4.   "Enhanced Security Policies and Procedures." *BNY Mellon.* n.d. Web. <*http://www.bnymellon.com/tapequery/security.html*>

5.   Adapted from "Statistics About Leading Causes of Data Loss."

6.   "Statistics About Leading Causes of Data Loss." *Protect-Data.com.* n.d. Web. Mar. 2011. <*http://www.protect-data.com/information/statistics. html*>

7.   Adapted from "Statististic About Leading."

8.   Zoladz, Chris. "Why PCI Compliance is so Confusing: you too can Take Charge!" *NYMITY,* Feb. 2011. Web. Mar. 2011. <*http://www. nymity.com/Free_Resources/Privacy_Interviews/2011/2011_Chris_ Zoladz.aspx?*>

9.   Adapted from "Enhanced Security Policies and Procedures."

10. BNY Mellon, n pag.

From my column the month this research note was published: "There's no doubt that leaning out organizations over the past four years has caused more work to have been done by fewer people. If we look at the controls structure inside a business, we see that controls have often been simplified or ignored, thus significantly reducing any "checks and balances" approach to risk. Plans to automate certain controls, particularly in the security area, have been put on hold because the funds are not available. When controls stay manual, they are performed by people who may or may not feel respected and supported in their work. Risk from events such as those described in our research note rises exponentially."

Navigating the Distinctive Challenge of Insider Crime

Andrew H. R. Hansen
November 2011

Introduction

Information security has often been referred to as a journey, not a destination. It's understandable that those committed to this journey often get focused on the hardware and software, malware and spyware, the network and firewall. With so much energy spent defending against threats perpetrated by those outside the organization, flying quietly under the radar is a threat easy to underestimate: employees inside the organization. Due to the fact that employees have legitimate access to information systems, networks and data warehouses, employees pose a risk to organizational security that should be taken seriously. This article will discuss major categories of employee crime, help employers identify suspicious behaviors and understand perpetrator motives, as well as recommend actions organizations should take to prepare for and respond to this inescapable vulnerability.

Types of Insider Crime

Unfortunately for information security professionals and their employers, types of insider crime are only limited by the imagination of the perpetrators. In an effort to narrow the scope to common criminal behaviors, we will focus on three major categories of insider crime defined by researchers at the Community Emergency Response Teams (CERT) and the Software Engineering Institute and CyLab at Carnegie Mellon University: fraud, theft of information, and IT sabotage.[1]

Fraud

Depending on the context, fraud can be defined in multiple ways. But reaching across the majority of characterizations is the simple, succinct, defining attribute: deception. Fraud is deception.[2] In a comprehensive report published by the Association of Certified Fraud Examiners (ACFE) in 2010, researchers compiled data from 1,843 cases of occupational fraud that occurred between January 2008 and December 2009.[3] For the purposes of their study, fraud was parsed into three general categories:

1. **Corruption** – Included behaviors like conflicts of interest (purchasing schemes, sales schemes, etc.), bribery (invoice kickbacks, bid rigging), illegal gratuities, and economic extortion

2. **Asset Misappropriation** – Included behaviors like larceny, skimming, fraudulent disbursements (billing schemes, payroll schemes, check tampering, ghost employee, commission schemes, workers compensation, forged endorsement, etc.)

3. **Fraudulent Statements** – Included behaviors like Asset/Revenue overstatements, timing differences, fictitious revenues, concealed liabilities and expenses, improper disclosures, improper asset valuation etc.[4]

The resulting statistics from this study indicate that government organizations and both public and private companies, are all experiencing increases in the frequency of fraud relative to 2008 figures.[5]

Not only is the rate of fraudulent incidents the highest amongst private and public companies, these organizations were also "victim to the costliest schemes… the median loss for the cases of these businesses was $231,000 and $200,000, respectively."[6] Losses experienced by government agencies and not-for-profit organizations were about half as much at $100,000 and $90,000 each.[7] Also worth noting, small businesses – defined as those with less than 100 employees – "suffered the greatest percentage of the frauds… accounting for more than 30% of the victim organizations."[8]

Theft of Information

Defined simply as "stealing confidential or proprietary information from the organization,"[9] theft of information can result in "loss of intellectual property, compromised customer privacy, loss of company reputation, and exposure to regulatory violations."[10] In a recent case of information fraud, an employee of a major bank sold private customer data to criminals. These transactions resulted in losses of $10 million dollars to the bank, and eroded trust between the bank and its customers.[11]

Research conducted by the Poneman Institute in 2009, "surveyed 945 adult-aged participants located in the US who were laid-off, fired or changed jobs in the last 12 months."[12] The study found that more than 59 percent of those surveyed claimed that they kept company data after leaving their employer, despite the fact that 79 percent acknowledge knowing "they do not have permission to do so."[13] The most prominent type of confidential, sensitive or proprietary information kept by the exiting employee was email lists, as 53 percent felt "the information might be useful to them in the future,"[14] followed by non-financial business information, customer information including contact lists, employee records, and financial information.[15]

IT Sabotage

IT sabotage is "acting with intention to harm a specific individual, the organization, or the organization's data, systems, and/or daily business operations."[16] In a study conducted by researchers with the United States Secret Service and CERT, of the insiders that had committed IT sabotage, "eighty-six percent of the insiders held technical positions."[17] Because employees are so familiar with the data and systems they work with on a regular basis, they often know the precise way to inflict the most severe damage to the organization. The study reported that financial losses associated with IT sabotage "ranged from a reported low of $500 to a reported high of 'tens of millions of dollars.'"[18]

In addition to financial damages caused to an organization, the following examples from an Insider Threat Study[19] conducted by CERT highlight problems associated with IT sabotage. These problems can include:

- "Severed communication with affected organizations due to shut-down networks, router, servers, or dial-up access

- Blocked sales due to inaccessible sales applications or deleted sales records

- Blocked customer contact due to blocked customer passwords

- Damaged or destroyed critical information assets, such as proprietary software, data, computing systems, and storage media necessary to the organization's ability to work, produce product, or develop new products

- Damaged supervisory integrity, including exposed personal or private communications embarrassing to a supervisor."[20]

Identifying Motives and Signals

For a variety of reasons, employers may feel that they are impervious to insider crime. They might mistakenly believe that their business has too few employees, their watchful eye has everything sufficiently covered, or that relationships have long been established as trusting. Findings from a comprehensive study prepared by the Association of

Certified Fraud Examiners (ACFE), point out that "eight-six percent (of perpetrators) had never been charged with or convicted of a prior offense."[21] This detail highlights the need for employers to be aware of common motives of internal crime and understand ways environmental circumstances influence these behaviors.

Developed by Dr. Donald R. Cressey, "The Fraud Triangle"[22] specifies three elements that are generally believed to be found in the majority of fraud cases. Although the model was based upon cases of fraud, the concepts certainly extend to the other types of employee crimes previously discussed. The three elements of the fraud triangle are:

1. Opportunity. For fraud to occur, the employee must believe the crime can be committed and concealed

2. Pressure. In many cases it is financial pressure, job dissatisfaction or fear of losing a job

3. Rationalization. Most often comes in the form of entitlement, or an inflated sense of self-importance and contributions, or a false sense of ownership.[23]

24

It is important for employers to recognize that the majority of insider crime is the direct result of a specific event or a series of events[25] – often the employee feels as though they have been mistreated in some way. Employees involved in insider crime almost always engage in some form of abnormal behaviors that comes to the attention of their coworkers.[26] However, abnormal behaviors should not necessarily be interpreted as extreme behaviors. Employers should watch for more basic changes in employee performance. For example, a generally strong performing and reliable employee is suddenly constantly truant or tardy, engages in arguments with coworkers, or the quality of their work diminishes significantly.[27] Each of these may be warning signs that the employee has been involved in an event that is negatively impacting their feelings towards their work.

Mitigating

Having covered major types of insider crime and identified some of the motives and behaviors associated with them, we are now better prepared to discuss possible mitigating steps employers can take to improve their ability to defend against these troubling actions.

In the study conducted by U. S. Secret Service and the Cert Program mentioned earlier, researchers suggested that "First, managers should recognize the personal predisposition of their employees and understand the impact they can have on insider threat risk. Second, organizations should attempt to manage expectations of employees to minimize unmet expectations."[28] Operating under this framework, employers are then better prepared to take further proactive mitigating steps.

Employers should strive to have clearly established policies in place, and ensure efforts have been made to educate and inform their employees. Conducting thorough pre-employment screenings can also serve as a layer of protection to the organization.[29] Employers should take the time to confirm that the people they are inviting to become a part of the organization are truly of the caliber they are expecting.

Efforts should also be made to ensure that there are open lines of communication between the different layers of the organization. Managers should not separate themselves from employee concerns, they should be willing to discuss grievances and make a special effort to resolve feelings of injustice or mistreatment.[30] Establishing a formal process for reporting incidents and documenting problematic behavior is also a wise practice.[31]

Lastly, "separation of duties is the most fundamental, effective fraud prevention measure. No single employee should have complete control over an entire transaction."[32] Although financial circumstances may make it difficult at times, implementing a system where multiple employees handle different tasks of the same transaction, can serve as a built in monitoring feature, and end up saving the employer money in the long run.

Like most threats to organizations, there is no panacea when it comes to dealing with insider crime. Employers should consider conducting a high-level audit of their own to brainstorm ways their organization might be vulnerable and prepare ways to mitigate these threats.

Responding to Suspected Insider Crime

Should an employer suspect criminal behavior, they should avoid jumping to conclusions. A thorough investigation should be conducted, being careful not to make accusations until actual evidence is found.[33] If an employee begins acting suspiciously or if credible evidence emerges in the investigation, employers should consider placing the employee on leave until after the investigation concludes.[34] Employers should also take special care to create detailed documentation throughout the entire process.[35]

Following these guidelines will increase the probability that an organization will be sufficiently protected against possible legal complications and improve their ability to press charges if this is deemed the appropriate course of action. Responding to insider crime in a measured and deliberate manner further protects the organization and ensures that a management misstep doesn't come back to cause additional harm to the organization.

Conclusion

Taking a moment to step outside all the statistics and recommendations allows the dust to settle on perhaps the most critical factor – the importance of open channels of communication and proper employee treatment. Hopefully the merit of this statement has been firmly grasped as these ideas have been alluded to throughout this article. The simple reality is that organizations would not exist without people. As previously established, the majority of insider crimes are caused by employees who feel they have been wronged or mistreated. Employers that take special notice and care to foster a responsive environment sensitive to the concerns of their employees will result in a healthier organization, better prepared to avoid the devastating consequences of insider crime.

References

1. Cappelli, Dawn M. "Pay Attention! What are Your Employees Doing?" Software Engineering Institute, Carnegie Melon University: 2006. Slide 11. Web. Nov. 2011. <*www.cert.org/archive/pdf/sepg500.pdf*>

2. Mieke Jans, Nadine Lybaert and Koen Vanhoof. "A Framework for Internal Fraud Risk Reduction at IT IntegratingBusiness Processes: The IFR^2 Framework." *The International Journal of Digital Accounting Research* 9, (2009) p. 3. Web. Nov. 2011. <*http://www.uhu.es/ijdar/10.4192/1577-8517-v9_1.pdf*>

3. "Report to the Nations on Occupational Fraud and Abuse," 2010 Global Fraud Study, *Association of Certified Fraud Examiners*, p. 4.

4. "Report to the Nations," 7.

5. "Report to the Nations," 27.

6. "Report to the Nations," 27.

7. "Report to the Nations," 27.

8. "Report to the Nations," 27.

9. Capelli, Slide 11.

10. "Theft of Information: A Multilayered Prevention Strategy," *Cisco*, n.d. Web. 7 Nov. 2011. <*http://www.cisco.com/en/US/solutions/ns170/networking_solutions_products_genericcontent0900aecd8051f382.html*>

11. David Lazarus. "Bank of America Data Leak Destroys Trust." *Los Angeles Times*, 24 May. 2011. Web. 7 Nov. 2011. <*http://articles.latimes.com/2011/may/24/business/la-fi-lazarus-20110524*>

12. "Data Loss Risks During Downsizing." *Poneman Institute, LLC.* Sponsored by Symantec Corporation. 23 Feb. 2009, p. 2.

13. "Data Loss Risks," 3-4.

14. "Data Loss Risks," 8,10.

15. "Data Loss Risks," 10.

16. Cappelli, Slide 11.

17. Cappelli, Dawn M., Andrew P. Moore and Randall F. Trzeciak. "The 'Big Picture' of Insider IT Sabotage Across U.S. Critical Infrastructures." *Software Engineering Institute*, Carnegie Melon, May, 2008. p. 3.

18. Cappelli, Moore, Trzeciak, p, 4.

19. Cappelli, Dawn M., Michelle Keeney, Eileen Kowalski, Stephanie Rogers, Timothy Shimeall. "Insider Threat Study: Computer Systems Sabotage in Critical Infrastructure Sectors." *Software Engineering Institute,* Carnegie Melon, May, 2005. p. 21.

20. Cappelli, et al, p. 21.

21. "Report to the Nations," 69.

22. "Employee Fraud and Embezzlement." *The Business Owner.* Control System Integrators Association. 30 (2006): p. 3.

23. "Employee Fraud," p. 3.

24. Image adapted from "Employee Fraud and Embezzlement."

25. Cappelli, Dawn, Tara Conway, Susan Keverline, Eileen Kowalski, Andrew Moore, Megan Williams, Bradford Willke. "Insider Threat Study: Illicit Cyber Activity in the Government Sector." *Software Engineering Institute,* Carnegie Melon, Jan, 2008. p. 14.

26. Cappelli, Conway, et al, p. 14.

27. "Employee Fraud," p. 7.

28. Cappelli, Moore, Trzeciak, p. 14.

29. "Employee Fraud," p. 4.

30. Cappelli, Keeney, Shimeall, p. 22.

31. Cappelli, Keeney, Shimeall, p. 23.

32. "Employee Fraud," p. 4.

33. "Employee Fraud," p. 6.

34. "Employee Fraud," p. 6.

35. "Employee Fraud," p. 6.

Still another area we've been tracking since 2009 is the advent of cloud computing, including the emergence of the Cloud Security Alliance and its Trusted Cloud project, as well as other resources including an excellent white paper from the National Institute of Standards and Technology. In a column in May of 2010, I noted that "It's cheaper to store your corporate data on the Internet, but what are the risks as balanced against the cost savings? How will regulators perform examinations of such virtual environments? Can cloud be used as a safe and effective disaster recovery tool? Can we set up portable and mobile emergency operations centers using cloud?" Here Hansen provides a basic explanation of cloud computing, and discusses new and emerging threats to cloud platforms, including those operated by the federal government.

Cloud Computing and Cyber Threats

Andrew H. R. Hansen
December 2011

Introduction

Renowned scholar, consultant and author Warren G. Bennis once published an article in which he quoted legendary hockey player Wayne Gretzky as saying, "It's not where the puck is, it's where the puck will be."[1] Imitating this statement, over the past two decades businesses have chased the rapidly advancing trends in technology with the hopeful intent of correctly projecting where technology – and subsequently, the profits – will be. One particular trend that has been gaining traction and appears to have staying power is cloud computing. This article will outline the basics of cloud computing, identify the major frameworks, discuss the cloud decision and describe several cyber threats associated with cloud computing.

Cloud Computing Basics

Whether they realize it or not, the majority of Internet users have already participated in cloud computing.[2] Examples of common cloud computing behaviors include accessing web-based email, participating in discussion forums or social networking, or using photo sharing websites.[3] The basic theory behind cloud computing is that alternative to storing and retrieving data on our own computers, that same data can be stored on a computer in the "cloud," making it accessible for any device with Internet access.[4] The term "cloud" originated in the early days of network design. As network engineers started connecting to networks outside of their domain, they realized they lacked the details of these outside networks.[5] "They needed a way to indicate that there is a network, but also indicate that they weren't trying to describe it, that it was more than they know. They landed on the cloud as a symbol of this unknown domain."[6]

For the standard web user, cloud computing will offer an array of enticing possibilities. "Imagine being able to share... photos, movies, contacts, e-mails, documents etc. – with your friends, family, and coworkers in an instant."[7] In a business context, cloud computing offers different but equally intriguing opportunities. Harvard Business Review describes the potential business benefits in this way,

> "Rather than house your own IT servers or rent the maximum processing and storage capacity

you'll ever need, why not pay only for what you use, when you use it? That's the basic idea behind cloud computing – and it's an alluring possibility for many reasons, not least the desire to contain costs and reduce energy consumption."[8]

According to the first Cisco Global Cloud Index, global cloud computing traffic is expected to rise an astonishing 1200 percent by 2015.[9] One major organization that will likely contribute to this statistic is the United States Federal government, who recently instated a "cloud first policy... Intended to accelerate the pace at which the government will realize the value of cloud."[10] Researcher Robert L. Grossman at the University of Illinois at Chicago echoes some of the positive implications of cloud computing mentioned above by claiming the increased focus on cloud computing has been fueled by three important factors: scalability, simplicity, and pricing.[11] Each of these attributes has the potential to give an organization a competitive advantage.

Included in the discussion of basic cloud computing, concepts, the difference between private and hosted clouds should also be illuminated. A private cloud is "devoted to a single organization's internal use; it might be run by the organization itself or outsourced to a third party to operate."[12] Whereas a public or hosted cloud is "managed by another organization that provides cloud services to a variety of third-party clients."[13] Hybrids of these cloud frameworks can also be implemented.

Cloud Computing Frameworks

Although the precise number of cloud frameworks varies depending on the source, in their book "Cloud Security and Privacy," industry experts Tim Mather, Subra Kumaraswamy and Shahed Latif identify a "commonly agreed upon framework for describing cloud computing services," which goes by the acronym "SPI."[14] SPI stands for Software-as-a-Service (SaaS), Platform-as-a-Service (PaaS) and Infrastructure-as-a-Service (IaaS).[15] The services offered by each of these frameworks will be discussed below.

Software-as-a-Service (SaaS)

Under the SaaS model, the customer will bypass the traditional purchasing of a software license agreement, and instead they will essentially rent a subscription or get pay-per-use access to software in the cloud.[16] A Customer Relationship Management service like SalesForce is a good example of SaaS.[17] Some characteristics of SaaS include:

- A typical SaaS deployment does not require any additional hardware and can be run via a web browser

- Through outsourcing, the cost of application software licensing, servers, and other infrastructure and personnel costs are reduced

- SaaS enables software vendors to control and limit use, and prohibit the illegal copying and distribution of their software.[18]

Platform-as-a-Service (PaaS)

In a PaaS model, "the vendor offers a development environment to application developers, who develop applications and offer those services through the provider's platform."[19] Windows Azure from Microsoft is a good example of the PaaS model.[20] Additional characteristics of PaaS include:

- Developers use pre-defined blocks of code and the vendor's development environment to create applications

- Offers general developers the ability to build web applications without needing specialized expertise

- Developers can often build web applications without installing any tools on their computer

- Provides a low cost entry, which greatly increases the number of applications created.[21]

Infrastructure-as-a-Service (IaaS)

IaaS has been compared to utility computing, as the service provider provides the infrastructure and the customer pays for the actual amount of processing power, disk space, etc. that they actually consume.[22] "From the IaaS provider's perspective, it can build an infrastructure that handles the peaks and troughs of its customers' demands and add new capacity as the overall demand increases."[23] Amazon's Elastic Compute Cloud is an example of this model.[24]

Additional characteristics of IaaS include:

- The ability to scale infrastructure needs in near-real-time based upon usage requirements

- Customers can purchase the exact amount of infrastructure required at any specific time

- In some cases the IaaS vendor will provide application support, application development, and enhancements

- Access to high quality IT talent for a fraction of the cost.[25]

The Cloud Decision

Each of the three frameworks described above have the ability to provide unique advantages to business of all sizes. But the decision to move to the cloud is not one that should be taken lightly. Business managers and others considering moving to the cloud should take the time to understand which model and which types of services would best suit their business needs. Possible good candidates for moving to the cloud might include a small-to-medium-sized business with a distributed workforce, or a business with customers that need to access their growing databases. Smaller businesses may find that the costs of supporting multiple servers and the IT expertise required to manage them is reduced by a move to the cloud. Similarly, a growing business with a rapidly expanding sales team might be a good candidate for a cloud-based application that manages their clientele.

Companies should not be afraid to start small. "Cloud computing is a different way of working from what most people are used to, and building familiarity and trust takes time."[26] Starting small with a pilot program, before moving forward with a full implementation is likely a wise strategy.

Further, organizations should not force their business strategy to fit into the cloud models. Alternatively, "consider what type of cloud would best fit your current operations and enhance your IT strategy."[27]

Security Concerns

While there are definitely benefits associated with cloud computing, there are also undeniable security concerns that need to be considered before businesses move sensitive information into the cloud. Researcher and author Michael Gregg recommends some useful questions businesses should ask when selecting a cloud service provider. The following suggested questions and explanations are taken directly from his 2010 report, "10 Security Questions for Cloud Computing."[28]

> **Where's the data?** Different countries have different requirements and controls placed on access. Because your data is in the cloud, you may not realize that the data must reside in a physical location. Your cloud provider should agree in writing to provide the level of security required for your customers.

> **Who has access?** Access control is a key concern, because insider attacks are a huge risk. A potential hacker is someone who has been entrusted with approved access to the cloud... Anyone considering using the cloud needs to look at who is managing their data and what types of controls are applied to these individuals.

> **What is the long-term viability of the provider?** How long has the cloud provider been in business and

what is their track record? If they go out of business, what happens to your data?

What happens if there is a security breach? If a security incident occurs, what support will you receive from the cloud provider? While many providers promote their services as being unhackable, cloud-based services are an attractive target to hackers.

What is the disaster recovery/business continuity plan? While you may not know the physical location of your services, it is physically located somewhere. All physical locations fact threats such as fire, storms, natural disasters, and loss of power. In case of any of these events, how will the cloud provider respond, and what guarantee of continued services are they promising?[29]

Cyber Threats

If the trend of businesses moving to the cloud continues as projected, expect hackers and their malicious attacks to follow. The cost of cybercrime to the global economy is estimated at $1 trillion dollars.[30] Cloud computing is not impervious to this criminal activity. Like any networked system of computers, cloud services are susceptible to things like denial of service (DoS) attacks, side channel attacks and man-in-the-middle attacks.[31] Researchers at the Cloud Computing Alliance, point out some cyber threats particularly challenging to those in the cloud computing industry. The following five threats and explanations have been taken from their report, "Top Threats to Cloud Computing."[32]

Insecure Interfaces – From authentication and access control to encryption ad activity monitoring, these interfaces must be designed to protect against both accidental and malicious attempt to circumvent policy.

Malicious Insiders – This threat is amplified for consumers of cloud services by the convergence of IT services and customers under a single management domain, combined with a general lack of transparency into provider process and procedure.

Shared Technology Issues – IaaS vendors deliver their services in a scalable way by sharing infrastructure. Often, the underlying components that make up this infrastructure were not designed to offer strong isolation properties for a multi-tenant architecture.

Data Loss or Leakage – There are many ways to compromise data. Deletion or alteration of records without backup of the original content is an obvious example. Unlinking a record from a larger context may render it unrecoverable, as can storage on unreliable media.

Account or Service Hijacking – Account or service hijacking is not new. Attack methods such as phishing, fraud, and exploitation of software vulnerabilities still achieve results. Credentials and passwords are often reused, which amplifies the impact of such attacks.[33]

Remediation

Fortunately, the Cloud Security Alliance has also provided a series of remediating protocols that can assist in mitigating these threats. These recommendations include:

- Analyze the security model of cloud provider interfaces Ensure strong authentication in concert with encrypted transmission

- Enforce strict supply chain management and conduct a comprehensive supplier assessment

- Require transparency into overall information security and management practices, as well as compliance report

- Implement security best practices for installation/configuration

- Monitor environment for unauthorized changes/activity

- Encrypt and protect integrity of data in transit

- Implement strong key generation, storage and management, and destruction practices

- Prohibit the sharing of account credentials between users and services.[34]

Businesses should seek out sufficient education related to the particular threats and remediation protocols associated with the framework and services they have selected. This begins by researching and becoming intimately familiar with the cloud service provider.

Taking the time to confirm that the service provider is appropriately meeting expectations will better ensure the probability of having secure and readily accessible information in the cloud.

Conclusion

Cloud computing is going to be a particularly interesting trend to follow. If projections are correct, the future of computing is in the cloud. Businesses should take the time to research the three primary frameworks of cloud computing and move forward responsibly and in accordance with their IT strategy. Although the cloud appears to offer many enticing characteristics, like any network of computers, it is also susceptible to malicious activities that pose a potential threat to information security. Businesses should take the time to become very familiar with the threats and remediation protocols associated with the cloud services they have selected to ensure that their business is able to continue operations safely and profitably into the future.

References

1. Bennis, Warren G. "Leadership in Change." *Breaking the Code of Change*. Micheal Beer and Nitin Nohria. Boston, MA: Harvard Business School Press, 2000. p. 116-117. Print.

2. Rivka, Tadjer. "What is Cloud Computing?" PCMag.*com*. 18 Nov. 2010. Web. 5 Dec. 2011. <*http://www.pcmag.com/ article2/0,2817,2372163,00.asp*>

3. Polrid. "Will Cloud Computing Feature Heavily in Forecasts for 2010?" *Technobuffalo.com*. 2 Jan. 2010. Web 5 Dec. 2011. <*http://www. technobuffalo.com/internet/will-cloud-feature-heavily-in-forecasts-for-2010/*>

4. Alexander, Stephen. "Cloud Computing to Grow 1200% by 2015." *Technoratio.com*. 29 Nov. 2011. Web. 6 Dec. 2011. <*http://technorati. com/technology/cloud-computing/article/cloud-computing-to-grow-1200-by/*>

5. Stevenson, Dennis. "Why is it Called the Cloud?" *Toolbox.com*. 24 Mar. 2009. Web. 6 Dec. 2011. <*http://it.toolbox.com/blogs/original-thinking/ why-is-it-called-quotcloud-computingquot-30713*>

6. Stevenson, n. pag.

7. Tadjer, n. pag.

8. "What We're Watching in Cloud Computing." *Harvard Business Review: The Magazine.* June, 2010. n. pag. Web. 6 Dec. 2011. <*http://hbr.org/2010/06/what-were-watching-in-cloud-computing/ar/1*>

9. Alexander, n. pag.

10. Kundra, Vivek. "Federal Cloud Computing Strategy." *CIO.gov.* United States Federal Government. p. 2. 8 June. 2011. Web. 6 Dec. 2011. <*http://www.cio.gov/documents/federal-cloud-computing-strategy.pdf*>

11. Grossman, Robert. "The Case for Cloud Computing." *Cloud Computing.* University of Illinois at Chicago: 2009. p.24. Web. 6 Dec. 2011. <*http://www.cmlab.csie.ntu.edu.tw/~freetempo/CN2011/hw/hw1/04804045.pdf*>

12. Grossman, p. 24.

13. Grossman, p. 24.

14. Kumaraswamy, Subra, Shahed Latif and Tim Mather. "Cloud Security and Privacy: An Enterprise Perspective on Risks and Compliance." California: O'Reilly Media, Inc. 2009. p. 11.

15. Kumaraswamy et al., p. 11.

16. Kumaraswamy et al., p. 18.

17. Singh, Basant N. "SaaS Introduction With Examples – Cloud Service Model." *Cloud Computing.* 26 April. 2010. Web. 6 Dec. 2011. <*http://www.techno-pulse.com/2010/04/saas-introduction-example-cloud-service.html*>

18. Kumaraswamy et al., p. 18.

19. Kumaraswamy et al., p. 19.

20. Allen, Brendan and Tom Henderson. "First Look at Windows Azure." *NetworkWorld.* 20 June 2011. Web. 6 Dec. 2011. <*http://www.networkworld.com/reviews/2011/062011-microsoft-windows-azure-test.html*>

21. Kumaraswamy et al., p. 19-20.

22. Kumaraswamy et al., p. 22.

23. Kumaraswamy et al., p. 22.

24. Sourya. "Cloud Computing For Dummies: SaaS, PaaS, IaaS and all That Was." *CloudTweaks.com.* 15 Feb. 2011. Web. 6 Dec. 2011. <*http://www.cloudtweaks.com/2011/02/cloud-computing-for-dummies-saas-paas-iaas-and-all-that-was/*>

25. Kumaraswamy et al., p. 22.

26. Martin, James. "Should you Move Your Small Business to the Cloud?" *pcworld.com*. 29 Jan. 2010. Web. 6 Dec. 2011. *<http://www.pcworld. com/businesscenter/article/188173-2/should_you_move_your_small_ business_to_the_cloud.html>*

27. Liang, Sheng. *Smart Business*. 1 April 2011. Web. 6 Dec. 2011. *<http:// www.sbnonline.com/2011/04/sheng-liang/>*

28. Gregg, Michael. "10 Security Concerns for Cloud Computing." *Globalknowledge.com*. 2010. p. 4-5. Web. 6 Dec. 2011.*<http://viewer. media.bitpipe.com/1078177630_947/1268847180_5/WP_VI_10Securit yConcernsCloudComputing.pdf>*

29. Gregg, p. 4-5.

30. Allen and Henderson, n. pag.

31. Gregg, p. 5.

32. To view the complete report, visit here: *<https://cloudsecurityalliance. org/topthreats/csathreats.v1.0.pdf>*

33. "Top Threats to Cloud Computing." *Cloud Security Alliance*. Mar. 2010. p. 8-13. Web. 6 Dec. 2011. *<https://cloudsecurityalliance.org/topthreats/ csathreats.v1.0.pdf>*

34. "Top Threats," p. 8-13.

CHAPTER IV

EMERGING TRENDS

We've had our eye on social media platforms like Twitter and Facebook since the inception of ASA, both as an emerging trend for trusted communications; and as a cutting edge emergency management tool. In what is really a very early piece on the topic, Bhagwatwar looks here at the use of social media platforms to build brand.

Business Impacts of Social Media

Akshay Bhagwatwar
December 2010

The use of social media has intensified from just being a medium for sharing ideas, expression and opinions to a tool for marketing businesses. Businesses use social media and social networking websites as a tool for gaining deep customer insight and to facilitate consumer influence. The newly coined term 'social media marketing' describes the act of using social media by a business for marketing, sales, public relations and customer service.[1] For the customers too, social media provides an ideal platform to speak their mind and spread positive as well as negative information about a company with their friends. Customers are uploading the videos on YouTube, speaking out their minds through Twitter or Facebook, sharing the pictures through Flickr and sharing their experiences through blogs. The virality of this information is high, often reaching millions of people. It is this viral marketing that companies try to leverage upon. Marketers are getting a chance to go closer to customers than ever before and get their feedback.

Measuring the business impact of social media depends on how effectively the social media has been able to reach the target audience and if this has been able to generate any business for the company. With the number of users on Facebook or Twitter exceeding millions, these social networking websites are serving as an ideal platform for any company to reach its audience through use of targeted advertising and online customer groups.

An example of a company using social media efficiently to achieve the goal of reaching target audience and gradually generating business for the company is Comcast. In March 2008, Comcast launched a twitter account with the name 'comcasters' (*https://twitter.com/#!/comcast/comcasters*). There is a team headed by Frank Eliason, the Senior Director of National Customer operations, to manage this account.[2] It is believed that this Twitter account has been able to single handedly turn around the negative service reputation (at least online) simply by quickly responding to tweets about service issues.[3] This is believed to be more effective than improving traditional call center wait times.[4]

A recent study on the impact of social media on business marketing puts forward some interesting facts:

1. 34% of people find information about a product through search engine

2. 30% of people learn about a new product through social networking websites

3. 28% said messages about sales or special deal notifications resonate with them.

4. 87% trust a friend's recommendation over a critic's review.[5]

Social media and Web 2.0 have begun to transform the way businesses are communicating with their customers and vice versa. The comfort with which customers can share their thoughts and ideas with millions across the web, social media provides an excellent platform for companies to monetize their brand evangelists.[6] Brand evangelists are customers that are so excited about a product or service that they are willing to tell their friends, family and others about it. There is a great potential for opportunities to create brand awareness through use of social media. The critical step is to first engage people in marketing campaigns. The next step is to drive brand awareness by using creative and clever ideas based on customer interest patterns. Once the brand awareness has been created, then the company can publicize its new products and marketing events through the social media and make sure that the publicity messages reaches all the loyal customers.

Social media and social networking websites have also turned out to be an effective tool for creating awareness about pandemics. Centers for Disease Control and Prevention (CDC) (*http://www.facebook.com/CDC*) and U.S. Department of Health and Human Sciences (HSS) have been actively using their Facebook groups as a medium for creating awareness about diseases like H1N1, AIDS and so on. The Facebook group of CDC alone has more than 150,000 members. CDC has been actively using this group to spread awareness about pandemics like H1N1 and also as a tool to caution public about any spam myths in circulations about various diseases.

Whether it is the Facebook, LinkedIn, Twitter or any other online discussion form, people are communicating and are communicating faster than ever before. They are loving or hating products and are sharing their thoughts with friends and family members. Listening to and interacting with such customers will help personalize a company's brand and provide an easy medium of communication to the most vocal costumers. A well implemented social media marketing strategy has an impact on the business of the company that goes beyond just measurable or tangible benefits. Social media marketing is something that businesses are making a part of their strategic plans as they move into a new world where social interaction through web will be faster than ever before.

References

1. Cavoli, Brian. "Measuring the Influence of Social Media." *Digital Influence Group*. 13 June 2008. Web. Dec. 2009. <*http://www.slideshare. net/DigitalInfluence/business-impact-of-social-media*>

2. Reisner, Rebecca. "Comcast's Twitter Man." *Bloomberg Businessweek*. 13 Jan. 2009. Web. Dec. 2009. <*http://www.businessweek.com/managing/ content/jan2009/ca20090113_373506.htm*>

3. Reisner, n. pag.

4. Boylan, Mike. "Social Media's Positive Business Impact." *Robert Morris University*. 11 Nov. 2009. p. 6. Web. Dec. 2009. <*http://mikeboylan.com/ dropbox/SocialMedia.pdf*>

5. Leggatt, Helen. "Marketing in Social Media not Off-Putting to Users." *bizreport.com*. 6 Nov. 2009. Web. Dec. 2009. <*http://www.bizreport. com/2009/11/marketing_in_social_media_not_off-putting_to_users. html*>

6. Boylan, n. pag.

There's a reason that, for many years, corporations have issued the device – usually a Blackberry – for corporate mobile use. With that device, they can avoid a range of security concerns that pop up with personal devices. But it's hard for employees to understand why they just can't connect their smartphone device to the corporate network, especially when it looks as simple as finding a USB port to plug into. There's a real challenge that's presented itself to companies as they appeal to a younger generation of workers, impatient with some of the controls around company data. Here Oxenford explores the issues, and proposes five steps that a corporation can take when implementing a range of mobile devices into the corporate network.

Mobile Devices & Business Security Risks

Emily Oxenford
November 2010

Introduction

A rising area of discussion today is the topic of techno-logical convergence particularly in mobile devices. All over the world we have seen a tendency towards multiple communications mediums or platforms becoming more alike – overlapping in both their capabilities and uses. Previously, a mobile phone was simply a phone on the move – it was just for making calls. A camera was a separate device just for taking pictures. Slowly things like text messaging, address books, and voicemail were added, and then cameras were added into mobiles. In parallel, the PDA developed – allowing individuals, especially business users, to organize their days and information on the go. Now the mobile device du jour is the "smartphone," which is not only a mobile phone with all the above, but now has access to the Internet. This has changed the world.

An Emerging Threat

There is a wide range of emerging risks and threats to be considered as smartphones in particular penetrate further and further into the workplace. In general, the more features, software, and plug-ins a device or system has, the more opportunities exist for exploitation and security vulnerabilities.[1] A serious concern, though, is that the various security technologies, standards, and policies that have been developed for PCs often do not necessarily apply to mobile devices. This is a rapidly growing field with completely new tasks and issues to address. Mobile device security is critical yet it seems to be lacking. There are risks of malware, hacking, viruses, identity theft, malicious email, spamming text messages, downloadable software with Trojan viruses – the familiar list of risks goes on, many from the lessons learned from the PC experience.[2]

For enterprises, company data can now easily be present on mobile devices, and this presents the problem of company data that are not within the control of the corporation. Mobile devices with cameras, texting, and email capabilities have made it so that companies must consider the security of privacy and proprietary information in new ways.[3]

There are two types of data-states to be considered on a mobile device. "Data at rest" pertains to the physical security of the device, as well as the data stored on the device. The best practice here is to encrypt data on the mobile device using 128-bit encryption (although if the device is left unsecured and requires no password for access, in the event that it is stolen, encryption won't help much). "Data in flight" pertains to the mobile device using networks outside of the enterprise information technology department's control.[4]

Additionally, the explosion of mobile applications on smartphones has had an accompanying rise in security vulnerabilities – often similar to what was seen on PCs a few years back. "When using a BlackBerry, Android, iPhone or other smartphone, we tend to assume all the nifty Web apps on these devices are relatively secure. At the least, we expect that a lot of the painful security lessons we received on PCs a decade ago have been applied to today's phone apps... our assumptions have been wrong."[5] There is still a significant security gap. In fact, "Lanier and Zusman concluded that in the mobile phone Web app world there's a lack of guidance, standards and best practices for developers."[6] This should be of serious concern for all companies and security professionals, in addition to individuals.

Addressing the Issue – Or Not

As it has been seen before, similar to the earlier days of the Internet, technology is moving markedly more quickly than security, and probably will be for a while. Unfortunately the default security on smartphones is often greatly lacking. Some regulating happens through software/security updates and patches, perhaps one way industry "deals with it," though it is often up to the consumer to actually proceed with the update to secure their mobile device.

Smartphones are such a new technology that is evolving daily - this is difficult to keep up with from a security standpoint. With the proliferation of a multitude of mobile operating systems like the Symbian (Nokia), Android (Google), Blackberry (RIM), iOS (Apple) and Windows Mobile (Microsoft), it makes it very difficult to keep up with the various systems. Blackberry has a good reputation for being able to secure information in a business environment, but Apple and Google lag behind.[7]

Mitigating Risks

Preparing a company to face and survive through these security threats and risks is a daunting and ongoing task for anyone. At a higher level, a company is going to want to ensure that there are sufficiently broad policies in place to cover mobile devices – both company-owned and employee-owned (but dealing with corporate information, such as with company email). A business will also have to take a critical look at the role of mobile phones in their organization. How important are mobiles to the work that needs to get done? Who actually needs access? What features and functionality do they need, and what is just nice-to-have?

From a security policy perspective it does make sense to lock down on smartphones in particular, especially considering the differences between personal versus company-owned devices. Something that should be incorporated into policy would be that it really depends on what the mobile device is being used for in business terms. There are some legitimate cost/benefit analyses one can conduct to discern what sorts of controls need to be put in place (especially post-lockdown).[8] For example, there are often C-level executives who need to be able to track their email all the time, assuming an administrative assistant is not doing that already. One idea might be to treat mobile devices like system administrative permissions – identifying the users who have a legitimate need for them.

There are a number of methods an organization can try when attempting to integrate mobile devices into the workplace.

1. Initially, ban all smartphones on the network, keeping these devices from operating on the network while trying to assess the best policies and practices.

2. Reach out to the business-side to determine their needs and run a parallel effort to conduct a threat analysis centered on smartphones and mobile devices.

3. Provide and support an employee education program that would empower individuals and build a security-aware environment and culture for employees.

4. Consider implementing a policy that allows only Intranet and no Internet, with proxy-controlled Internet access only for approved business requirements.

5. Put a procedure in place to immediately lock smartphones out of the intranet should a zero day or significant malware attack take place.

As with any new technology, a firm will want to apply change management principles to determine if it is right for the company. Mobile technology has a lot of advantages for individuals but it exposes organizations to risk. Individuals cannot really be blamed for wanting to take advantage of these emerging technologies, and so organizations must create secure and clear messages about the expectations and policies.

References

1. Koprowski, Gene J. "Mobile Phone Converging With 'Flash', Other Apps." *TechnewsWorld.com*. 10 June 2006. Web. Nov. 2010. *<http://www.technewsworld.com/story/51011.html>*

2. McDowell, Mindi. "Defending Cell Phones and PDAs Against Attack." *US Computer Emergency Readiness Team*. 27 Jan. 2009. Web. Nov. 2010. *<http://www.us-cert.gov/cas/tips/ST06-007.html>*

3. Korzenioski, Paul. "Next-Gen Devices may Integrate Cellular, WiFi Connectivity." *TechNewsWorld*. 7 Sept. 2006. Web. Nov. 2010. *<http://www.technewsworld.com/story/52822.html>*

4. Brenner, Bill. "SecTor 2010: Touring (and Surviving) the Mobile app Minefield." *CSOonline*. 27 Oct. Web. Nov. 2010. *<http://www.csoonline.com/article/630265/sector-2010-touring-and-surviving-the-mobile-app-minefield>*

5. Brenner, n. pag.

6. Brenner, n. pag.

7. McDowell, Mindi. "Defending Cell Phones and PDAs Against Attack." *US Computer Emergency Readiness Team*. 27 Jan. 2009. Web. Nov. 2010. *<http://www.us-cert.gov/cas/tips/ST06-007.html>*

8. Tauschek, Mark. "Developing and Instituting Corporate Mobile Device Policies." *Searchmobilecomputing.com*. 9 Sept. 2008. Web. Nov 2010. *<http://searchmobilecomputing.techtarget.com/feature/Developing-and-instituting-corporate-mobile-device-policies>*

My column in the month that Oxenford wrote this research note was titled "Taming the Beast of Electronic Speech." With respect to Oxenford's recommendation that a social media policy be created, I noted in my column that "Creating a policy that covers electronic communications is a good way to remind all employees that confidential and proprietary information (trademarks, upcoming product releases, sales, finances, number of products sold, number of employees, company strategy or any other non-public information) may not be discussed or posted anywhere. A good policy would also note that any commentary on the company itself must include an identification of self as employee along with a disclaimer that one is not speaking for the company. Any electronic postings done on corporate computers must respect copyright, privacy, fair use, financial disclosure and any other applicable laws. Finally, the policy should remind employees that the company owns any communication sent on its computers or that is stored there, and has the right to access any of that material that is stored on your computer at any time."

Social Media, Employees & Workplace Concerns

Emily Oxenford
January 2011

Introduction

Social media and social networking are hot topics for businesses these days, and the pace of information sharing has been changed forever. Now with technologies and services ranging from Facebook, Twitter, LinkedIn, blogs, texting, instant messaging, Flickr – the list is ongoing and ever growing. These new modes of communication are now allowing for people to share immediate and unfiltered content. And this has raised many questions, debates, and problems for companies and organizations that are struggling to keep up with the pace and shifts that drive the dynamic world of electronic communications.

Social Media Concerns

Some of the concerns for a company around social media have to deal with employee behavior and information-sharing practice. There are a number of security, ethical, and legal concerns about employees using social media in the workplace. The emergence of social media within the workplace has created new and unprecedented scenarios, particularly with the newest batch of employees entering the work force. Particularly, as Robert Mason et al. point out, these emerging workers are people who have "grown up in a world surrounded by connectivity and digital tools."[1] They are 'net natives' or 'digital natives.' These are people who have never known a world without the Internet, instant messaging, online games, and the possibility of persistent digital presence with networks of people."[2]

There is a wide range of individual and corporate expectations and thoughts about what constitutes appropriate use of social media in the workplace. Is it acceptable to text while in a meeting? What about someone who accesses Facebook on company time and on company equipment? What about using those 140 characters on Twitter to make a frustrated comment about a supervisor, off time and off site? Sometimes it is simply organizational culture that dictates what is deemed acceptable in the online sphere. But regardless, "one thing … is that there is a certain lack of clarity on the part of employees about what's acceptable and what is not. The conclusion is that companies might want to establish policies or engage in a dialogue about this."[3] Depending on the sector and services, there are various levels of appropriate behavior by employees using social media. In some cases, it may be best to completely cut off access, and in others, full-blown company use of social media tools can actually contribute to customer service and add value.

Social Media in Context

Determining what concerns a company may have about social media usually is tied in to what kinds of services they provide. For example, some organizations may be concerned about their public image – their sales and revenue depend on keeping a positive competitive edge, and thoughtless employee commentary could damage that. Other companies, on the other hand, deal in sensitive, proprietary, and private information. Employers in financial institutions, legal firms, government offices, educational institutes, and medical facilities all must ensure that they protect their information and prevent the inadvertent disclosure of confidential information.[4] Employees must not Tweet about clients or patients, even if the story makes them laugh, nor share corporate decisions that are not yet made public.

Trouble has occurred when assumptions are made about what employees know - kinds of behavior and practices are acceptable and which are not. *Forbes* business magazine reports that significant damage to business and careers can be made in the milliseconds it takes to put something out into the cybersphere.[5] Sometimes managers and supervisors are left baffled, seeing younger employees behave online in unethical or simply rude ways.[6]

A Social Media Policy

At the end of the day, much of social media behavior and uses in the workplace is dependent on the organizational culture and the people who work there. But any company needs to place social media on the table and have company-wide dialogue. Policy should be created to fit the needs and culture of the organization. Ideally, because people watch and are influenced by each other, the behavior set by managers and supervisors will inform how their employees approach social media use. John Putzier says it well: "Traditional managers want [to have] a policy and be done with it, and that's not realistic and effective. Your whole philosophy should be, 'It depends.'"[7] But a policy is insufficient if it is not backed up by example and clear communication.

There is a legal area that a company must consider as well, to cover their own liability and employees. Any policy should explicitly call out that "the employer reserves and exercises the right to monitor all communications made using company property."[8] This is particularly important to ensure that the company does not violate any privacy laws that protect employee. Perhaps most importantly, employers should offer training to employees on the appropriate use of social media under any policy that is created.

Take Action

Organizations need to make social media practice a part of their company's official conversation. Social media use is no longer a water-cooler conversation, but a boardroom dialogue. Companies and managers need to be informed of what and how social media uses might violate legal or ethical policies, and then make sure all employees have that communicated to them. But they must be aware that simply having a policy will not necessarily change behavior. These policies have to be established, integrated, and accepted. Corporate culture, the "tone at the top" is often a powerful key to appropriate behavior being followed.

Managers and established employees should give new employees guidance and develop a culture of coaching for appropriate behavior. No one should make assumptions that new hires will know the practices and behavior expectations. Set the expectations and explain the rules the very first day of employment.

Also, employers can "urge employees to separate their personal and professional digital lives," says John Lanham.[9] While it may seem basic, employees need to hear from their managers they are prohibited from sharing any confidential information, regardless of method or venue. Using examples that are relevant to the company and work can help make this more clear and understandable.

Social media and the changes it is bringing to the work place are not going away. While clear precedent and policies are often shifting and changing, companies must develop plans and strategies to integrate into their culture and organization.

References

1. Mason, Robert M., Karine Barzilai-Nahon, and Nancy Lou. "The Organizational Impact of Digital Natives." *17ᵗʰ International Conference on Management of Technology.* April 2008. p. 1. Web. Jan. 2011. <*http://ekarine.org/wp-admin/pub/IAMOT_DN_2008.pdf*>

2. Mason, et al. p. 1.

3. Rafferty, Heidi Russell. "Social Media Etiquette: Communication Behavioral Expectations." *Society for Human Resource Management.* 24 Mar. 2010. Web. Jan. 2011. <*http://www.shrm.org/hrdisciplines/technology/Articles/Pages/SocialMediaEtiquette.aspx*>

4. Knowledge@Wharton. "Are you Practicing Proper Social Networking Etiquette?" *Forbes.com.* 9 Oct. 2009. Web. Jan. 2011. <*http://www.forbes.com/2009/10/09/social-networking-etiquette-entrepreneurs-management-wharton.html*>

5. Knowledge@Wharton, n. pag.

6. Krell, Eric. "The Great Divide – Social Media in Today's Workplace." *Big Fat Finance Blog.* 17 Aug. 2009. Web. Jan. 2011. <*http://bigfatfinanceblog.com/2009/08/17/the-great-divide-social-media-in-todays-workplace*>

7. Rafferty, n. pag.

8. Lanham, John R. "Social Media and the Workplace." *Employment Law Commentary, Morrison & Forester LLC 22, no. 1.* 2010. p. 1-7. Web. Jan 2011. <*http://www.jdsupra.com/post/documentViewer.aspx?fid=8fb861e8-22c2-456c-8a24-ded05701484b*>

9. Rafferty, n. pag.

As noted earlier in this volume, risks around data have been a research area for ASA since its inception, whether from inside threats or through the type of targeted attacks that Hansen is describing in this research note. One thing is sure: such attacks are only going to increase over the coming years. We are starting to see the formation of centers for information sharing of a different type than, for instance, the Financial Services Information Sharing & Assessment Center (FS-ISAC), perhaps because of the magnitude of the threats at this time. This is a risk topic ASA will continue to track.

Trends in Data Breaches

Andrew H. R. Hansen
January 2012

Introduction

Over the past half century Western culture has evolved from an industrial economy to a knowledge economy. We are now in the early stages of what some are referring to as the "creative economy."[1] Throughout these societal changes, our dependence upon technology – from both a business and personal perspective – has risen dramatically. With this increased reliance on technology, individuals, businesses and governments are gradually realizing the critical responsibility of protecting information. This article will reference recent security breaches to bring to attention trending information assurance concerns from a local and global perspective, as well as discuss possible ways to prepare for and mitigate these threats.

Hacktivism

One increasingly prevalent concern in information security is "hacktivism" – the "act of hacking, or breaking into
a computer system, for a politically or socially motivated
purpose."[2] Those who engage in hacktivism often belong
to hacking groups or communities. Anonymous and Lulz
Security (usually abbreviated LulzSec), are arguably the
most prominent of these hacking communities. Although
the motives of these two hacking groups may differ, they
have successfully exploited a diverse selection of targets,
including: major corporations, religious groups, social
networks, and governments. In October, 2011, hackers
from Anonymous claimed responsibility for removing
forty secret child pornography websites.[3]

Stratfor

With the aim of better understanding international events
and reducing risk,[4] Stratfor is an Austin, Texas, based security think tank and consulting firm that claims to provide
"an audience of decision-makers and sophisticated news
consumers in the U.S. and around the world with unique
insights into political, economic, and military develop-
ments."[5] They are also amongst the latest targets of an
Anonymous hack.

On December 24, 2011, members of Anonymous
claimed responsibility for "crashing the Web site of the
(Stratfor) group… pilfering its client list, e-mails and credit
card information in an operation they say is intended to
steal $1 million for donations to charity."[6] Although Strat-
for has not been extremely vocal in the debate regarding

transparency of information (illustrated in cases like WikiLeaks), Anonymous claims Stratfor was targeted as "subject of interest" due to the more vocal positions of Stratfor's clientele.[7]

The hacking group allegedly posted a list online that they claim contains "Stratfor's confidential client list as well as credit card details, passwords and home addresses for some 4,000 Stratfor clients."[8] Anonymous also claimed the portion of client information already posted online represented a fraction of the 200 gigabytes they stole from Stratfor.[9] The 200 gigabytes of data is reportedly mostly email, with the hacking group claiming to have obtained approximately 3 million emails.[10] Stratfor later denied the allegation that their private client list was compromised,[11] but surprisingly, the credit card details appeared to be unencrypted, "an easy-to-avoid blunder which, if true, would be a major embarrassment for any security-related company."[12]

Shortly after the breach donations to charities like the Red Cross, Save the Children and Care started to show up on the credit cards of Stratfor clients.[13] In an interview after the incident, Barrett Brown, the apparent public face to Anonymous, stated that the media focus on the credit card issues were certainly "newsworthy," but that the "original purpose and ultimate consequence of the operation has largely been ignored."[14] He went on to explain that the hack was not about the credit card information or client lists, rather:

> "The operation was pursued in order to obtain the 2.7 million e-mails that exist on the firm's servers. This wealth of data includes correspondence with

untold thousands of contacts who have spoken to Stratfor's employees off the record over more than a decade. Many of those contacts work for major corporations, within intelligence and military contracting sectors, government agencies, and other institutions for which Anonymous and associated parties have developed an interest..."[15]

The worst may still be ahead for Stratfor, as members of Anonymous sift through those emails attempting to find incriminating information. Meanwhile, false emails have been circulating claiming to originate from George Friedman, the political scientist, author and CEO of Stratfor, an action that required releasing a video warning message to Stratfor customers by Vice President Fred Burton on the company's YouTube page.[16] Stratfor's main website remained down for weeks and was finally made live again on January 11.[17]

Cyber Warfare

Cyber warfare "involves units organized along nation-state boundaries, in offensive and defensive operations, using computers to attack other computers or networks through electronic means."[18] Many nations, including the United States, have established formal cyber security teams. In 2011, the United States deployed a new cyber unit specifically geared towards "combating the millions of low-grade attacks targeting the nation's 15,000 networks and 7 million computers on a daily basis."[19]

The United States is not the only nation concerned about malicious cyber activities. China also recently organized a thirty member "Cyber Blue Team," tasked with defending against cyber-attacks.[20] In a similarly manner, Japan has partnered with Fujitsu Ltd., "one of its major technology giants, in developing a virus for tracking down the source of cyber attacks and for nullifying their effect."[21]

Stuxnet

Originally deployed in 2009, the computer worm known as Stuxnet has since rapidly launched to the forefront of the cyber warfare dialogue, and "may be the most sophisticated cyberweapon ever deployed."[22] Stuxnet started appearing in industrial programs around the globe, but as experts started dissecting it, they "soon determined that it had been precisely calibrated in a way that would send nuclear centrifuges wildly out of control, adding suspicion that it was meant to sabotage Iran's nuclear program."[23] The basic functionalities of the worm have been described thusly:

> "The worm itself now appears to have included two major components. One was designed to send Iran's nuclear centrifuges spinning wildly out of control. Another seems right out of the movies: The computer program also secretly recorded what normal operations at the nuclear plant looked like, then played those readings back to plant operators, like a pre-recorded security tape in a bank heist, so that it would appear that everything was operating normally while the centrifuges were actually tearing themselves apart."

It is believed that in its prime, Stuxnet was responsible for destroying "1,000 centrifuges at the Natanz fuel enrichment facility by sabotaging their motors."[24] Experts estimate Stuxnet potentially set Iran's nuclear development program back several years.[25] Not surprisingly, Iran has responded by embarking on an "ambitious plan to boost its offensive and defensive cyber-warfare capabilities and is investing $1 billion in developing new technology and hiring new computer experts."[26]

Chief amongst the mysteries that still surround Stuxnet is who developed it. Ed Byres, Chief Technology Officer for Byres Security, estimated it would take months, if not years, of coding to make Stuxnet operate like it did.[27] Combining the complexity of the code with the fact that nearly sixty percent of infected machines were located in Iran[28] and most experts will agree that this is most certainly the work of a nation state.[29] The most prominent theory points to the mounting evidence that suggests Stuxnet is the product of collaboration primarily between the United States and Israel.[30] Both countries formerly deny these allegations, however, "Israeli officials grin widely when asked about its (Stuxnet's) effects."[31] In a 2011 conference concerning Iran, Gary Samore, chief strategist for combating weapons of mass destruction for the United States sidestepped a question about Stuxnet, but then said with a smile, "I'm glad to hear they are having problems with their centrifuge machines, and the U.S. and its allies are doing everything we can to make it more complicated."[32]

Handling Hacktivism

These trends may appear unrelated, but they share the common threads of both being manifestations of targeted attacks and products of political discord. Targeted attacks, like the one illustrated in the Stratfor case, are expected to rise in 2012.[33] By leaving their sensitive customer data unencrypted, Stratfor is a prime example of a high profile, sophisticated organization, failing to comply with basic security practices. "Mitigating exposure of your accounts and systems to hacktivism (or hacking in general) should always be a part of a comprehensive security strategy."[34] Some additional precautions organizations can take include:

- Limiting access to your corporate social media accounts to specific personnel and govern them with policy and password enforcement

- Use a web content filtering system to limit downloading of malware

- Ensure that web servers and public-facing portals are protected behind an active intrusion-prevention system or firewall that actively scans uploaded and downloaded content.[35]

Organizations should regularly review their security practices and policies to ensure there are no gaps in security and that the organization is keeping pace with advancing trends.

Dealing With Disruption

Although the thought of cyber warfare may seem distant and unlikely, the probability that businesses will face some form of disruption in normal operations increases with the constant unrest in the global political climate. It may be wise to pause and consider alternative ways of implementing business practices should a major disruption of systems occur. Researchers at New York University identified three primary ways communications are disrupted in a disaster, they include:

- Physical destruction of network components
- Disruption in supporting network infrastructure
- Network congestion.[36]

Dedicating the resources to research each of these three forms of disruption and building remediation protocols that deal specifically with the unique consequences of each type, will better prepare the organization for recovery should a major catastrophe or act of cyber warfare occur.

Conclusion

As society becomes increasingly dependent on technology, the need for individuals, businesses and governments to implement information security practices is no longer an optional decision. With political unrest becoming a constant factor, targeted attacks like hacktivism and cyber warfare will become more common occurrences. Fortunately, these threats are often manageable if appropriate policy, controls and remediation protocols are put in place. Organizations need to research the specific challenges they may face and prepare alternative courses of action in preparation for major disruptions in normal operations.

References

1.   Plooy, Peter du. "Narrowing the Gap Within Different Generations in the Workplace." *Management Exchange*. 31 Oct. 2011. Web. 5 Jan. 2012. <*http://www.managementexchange.com/ hack/narrowing-gap-within-different-generation-workplace*>

2. "Hacktivism." *SearchSecurity.* Web. 5 Jan. 2012 *<http:// searchsecurity.techtarget.com/definition/hacktivism>*

3. Liebowitz, Matt. "Anonymous Hackers Take Down Child Porn Websites, Leak Users' Names." *Security News Daily.* 20 Oct. 2011. Web. 5 Jan. 2012. *<http://www.securitynewsdaily.com/anonymous-hackers-child-porn-sites-1260/>*

4. Stratfor Global Intelligence. "Beware of False Communications." *YouTube.com.* 6 Jan. 2012. Web. 6 Jan 2012. *<http://www.youtube.com/ user/STRATFORvideo?feature=watch>*

5. Beware of False Communications, *YouTube.com.*

6. Perlroth, Nicole. "Hackers Breach the Web Site of Stratfor Global Intelligence." *The New York Times.* 25 Dec. 2011. Web. 5 Jan. 2012. *<http:// www.nytimes.com/2011/12/26/technology/hackers-breach-the-web-site-of-stratfor-global-intelligence.html?scp=1&sq=stratfor&st=cse>*

7. Durden, Tyler. "Anonymous Explains Why 2.7 Million Stratfor Emails Were Hacked." *ZeroHedge.* 27 Dec. 2011. Web. 2 Feb. 2012. *<http:// www.zerohedge.com/news/anonymous-explains-why-27-million-stratfor-emails-were-hacked>*

8. Perlroth, n.pag.

9. Vinograd, Cassandra and Ramit Plushnick-Masti. "'Anonymous' Hackers Target US Security Think Tank." *Yahoo! News.* 25 Dec. 2011. Web. 5 Jan. 2012 *<http://news.yahoo.com/anonymous-hackers-target-us-security-think-tank-190846242.html>*

10. Perlroth, Nicole. "Questions About Motives Behind Stratfor Hack." *The New York Times.* 27 Dec. 2011. Web. Jan 5. 2012. *<http://bits.blogs. nytimes.com/2011/12/27/questions-about-motives-behind-stratfor-hack/>*

11. Albanesius, Chloe. "Stratfor Denies Hack Included Access to 'Private Client' List." *Pcmag.com.* 27 Dec. 2011. Web. 5 Jan. 2012. *<http://www. pcmag.com/article2/0,2817,2398060,00.asp>*

12. Albanesius, n. pag.

13. Perlroth, "Hackers," n. pag.

14. Durden, n pag.

15. Durden, n pag.

16. Stratfor, YouTube.

17. O'Dell, Jolie. "Stratfor Site is Back Online After Recovering From

Anonymous Attack." *VentureBeat.* 11 Jan. 2012. Web. 2 Feb. 2012. <*http://venturebeat.com/2012/01/11/stratfor-is-back/*>

18. Billo, Charles G. and Welton Chang. "Cyber Warefare: An Analysis of the Means and Motivations of Selected Nation States." *Institute for Security Technology Studies at Dartmouth College.* Dec. 2004. Web. 5 Jan.   p. 3. 2012. <*http://www.ists.dartmouth.edu/docs/cyberwarfare.pdf*>

19. Pentland, William. "Still Recovering From Largest Cyber Attack on Record, U.S. Military Creates 'Cyber Unit.'" *Forbes.com.* 24 July. 2011. Web. 6 Jan. 2012. <*http://www.forbes.com/sites/williampentland/2011/07/24/still-recovering-from-largest-cyber-attack-on-record-u-s-military-creates-cyber-unit/*>

20. Agence France-Presse. "China Sets up Military Cyberwarfare Team: Report." *DefenseNews.com.* 27 May. 2011. Web. 6 Jan. 2012 <*http://www.defensenews.com/story.php?i=6644608*>

21. Kardare, Ankita. "Fujitsu Developing Virus to Combat Cyber Threats – Japan Government Funded Project." *Crazyengineers.com.* 2 Jan. 2012. Web. 6 Jan. 2012. <*http://www.crazyengineers.com/fujitsu-developing-virus-to-combat-cyber-threats-japan-government-funded-project-1540/*>

22. "Stuxnet." *The New York Times.* 15 Jan. 2011. Web. 6 Jan. 2012. <*http://topics.nytimes.com/top/reference/timestopics/subjects/c/computer_malware/stuxnet/index.html?inline=nyt-classifier*>

23. "Stuxnet," n. pag.

24. Katz, Yaakov. "Iran Embarks on $1 b. Cyber-warfare Program." *The Jerusalem Post.* 18 Dec. 2011. Web. 6 Jan. 2012. <*http://www.jpost.com/Defense/Article.aspx?id=249864*>

25. "Stuxnet," n. pag.

26. Katz, n. pag.

27. Zetter, Kim. "Blockbuster Worm Aimed for Infrastructure, But no Proof Iran Nukes Were Hit." *Wired.com.* 23 Sept. 2010. Web. 6 Jan. 2012. <*http://www.wired.com/threatlevel/2010/09/stuxnet/*>

28. Halliday, Josh. "Stuxnet Worm is the 'Work of a National Government Agency." *Theguardian.com.* 24 Sept. 2010. Web. 6 Jan. 2012. <*http://www.guardian.co.uk/technology/2010/sep/24/stuxnet-worm-national-agency*>

29. Allen, Ian. "Experts See Nation-State Behind Sophisticated Computer Virus Attack." *Intelnews.org.* 29 Sept. 2010. Web. 6 Jan. 2012. <*http://intelnews.org/2010/09/29/01-571/*>

30. Broad, William J., John Markoff and David E. Sanger. "Israeli Test on Worm Called Crucial in Iran Nuclear Delay." *The New York Times*. 15 Jan. 2011. Web. 6 Jan. 2012. <*http://www.nytimes.com/2011/01/16/world/middleeast/16stuxnet.html?pagewanted=all*>

31. Broad et al., n. pag.

32. Broad et al., n. pag.

33. Gonslaves, Antone. "10 Security Predictions for 2012." *Crn.com*. 26 Dec. 2011. Web. 6 Jan. 2012. <*http://m.crn.com/69730/show/c8379739 b3dec244f54a38ab1167382a&t=g6jgm2amio26v3801438oo6sn0*>

34. Byers, Cameron. "Hacktivism: How to Stay one Step Ahead of the Trend." *Astaro.com*. 14 Nov. 2011. Web. 6 Jan. 2012. <*http://www.astaro.com/blog/perspectives/hacktivism-how-to-stay-one-step-ahead*>

35. Byers, n. pag.

36. Moss, Mitchell L. and Anthony M. Townsend. "Telecommunications Infrastructure in Disasters: Preparing Cities for Crisis Communications." *New York University*. April. 2005. Web. 6 Jan. 2012. p. 4. <*http://www.nyu.edu/ccpr/pubs/NYU-DisasterCommunications1-Final.pdf*>

Made in the USA
Charleston, SC
03 May 2012